Think Nothing of Me

Shawnda Chambers

Dedicated to all the Lilith's,
waiting on the dark side of the moon

He doesn't smell the same as you do. And when he holds me his grip is just a little bit tighter. Perhaps it's because he knows I don't belong to him — this moment is fleeting. He is holding on because I might disappear. I put my head on his chest, noting that he must be a little bit shorter than you because if I move too suddenly I will bump his chin, whereas with you my cheek rests softly over your heart. Sometimes I would sit there, with my head on your heart. I'd just sit there and listen. Trying to hear the dripping valve, wondering if your defective heart was the reason you seem incapable of love. As if all of the love I poured into you slowly dripped out until it was gone.

Every fiber of my being is screaming out that this is wrong. If I hadn't, just moments before, tossed back a few drinks, I might be inclined to heed the steady, persistent warnings dancing in my head. As it is, I couldn't care less. In this moment I seek retribution. An eye for an eye. My right hand rubs my left. Notes the absence of my wedding band. Feels the loss and momentarily doesn't know what to do. The old habit of spinning my diamond back and forth will have to be replaced. But for now, there is nothing, and so the fingers hover and then fall.

Is glass fragile because it breaks? Are rubber bands elastic because they stretch? Do fish belong in water because they swim? Are you guilty because I caught you? If I hadn't, would you still be in the wrong? Simple rules of cause and effect. Metaphysical bullshit. All around me things are breaking: my favorite glass candle holders, my pretty little tea cup and saucer. Trinkets mean nothing. But the metaphor is there. My heart is breaking too — it's broken now. I see the connection and wait for the lesson. Strike the glass, watch it fall to the floor: it will end up broken. Shattered into a million pieces. I have caught you, found your faults. How about me? I haven't been caught. Am I any less responsible, remorseful, reprehensible? Will you shatter too? Your heart in a million pieces, on the floor, next to mine?

I am with you, but parts of me are gone. As I stand outside of this hotel room next to a man who is shorter than you, who doesn't smell like you and who will never ever love me, or, as it turns out, even look at me while we have sex, I wonder how I got here. How we got here. Why did you bring us here? All those vows. Broken. Infidelity crowds the space when we are alone now. I can think of nothing else. She has no face, only a name. But her presence. It suffocates me. I can never forget.

But tonight I will. For a little while, anyway. I flip my hair and kiss his cheek. Coy. He smiles because it is so easy. I have made it so easy. I will give him the parts of me that I took back from you. Because for now, I don't know yet what else to do with them.

"Did you come for this?" he asked me once while we were being intimate. I chose not to answer. Tried to ignore him. I didn't want to think about why I was here, when I should have been with you. But he persisted. Asking the same question over and over with growing intensity, forcing me to pay attention, to answer the question in my mind too. Why? My reasons were vengeful, hurtful, not at all like the beauty in the moment we were sharing. I pushed my face back into the leather seat of my car to keep myself quiet. So the words wouldn't escape. Because what I wanted to say needed to be left unspoken. And once again my thoughts returned to you — always back to you. He asked the question and silently I answered: "It's all because of you." I almost hate you now and I want you to hate me too. I'm tired of hearing you say you understand when really the only way to know is to feel it yourself. To experience the hurt on the same level I was forced to. Over and over. Without choice.

Because you chose. I did not. There were never any consequences for you. I took you back each and every time — except this last time. I feel dizzy with power. In this one moment I am able to make him feel good and make you feel bad. I have forgotten that for me too there will be consequences. But I am caught up in the lesson, the one I want to teach you. I swallow my anger and feel it rise, deep in my belly. Anger, mixing with pleasure. Pleasure mixing with anger until the two are inseparable. Rising and falling. Still he asks the question, only now it has been shortened and he pants "you came," over and over, almost with disbelief. He was right. For this. I came.

I don't think of him at all when he touches me now. I only think of you. In the moments when we are together, I'm not even there at all. Someone is, because the moment gets recorded. Recorded and replayed over and over again, consuming most of my days. But your big sad eyes, your disappointment in me, that's all I see at the time. I have to be careful not to say your name. When I share my body with him it connects me to you in a way I can't even explain. Perhaps it is in the emptiness I start to see in glimpses. Knowing the moments I share with him are temporal, but the ones I have with you forever. Is it strange to say that making love to another man makes me love you even more? Makes me ache for the connection we shared? Share, not shared — because I still feel it. Still feel you. Sometimes I whisper "I'm sorry" and don't even realize I have said it aloud until he looks at me, puzzled, asking what for. Now, I have to bite my tongue to keep from confessing to you. I hold back my apologies until they roll out of my eyes, down my cheeks. I name each tear as it falls. Blame. Guilt. Remorse. Shame. "I'm sorry," I whisper. But you don't hear me. Because to you, I don't say it aloud. Am careful not to.

I don't kiss and tell. But to you, I tell everything. I can't hold it inside anymore. I spill my secrets, I confess it all. I vomit the truth until it sits in front of us. I can still see your expression: the shock, the disbelief — and then the anger. Finally, there is anger. It rages out of your eyes. I wonder if you will hit me. Know that I deserve it. Almost hope you do it. But of course, you don't. You hurt me in other ways, but never physically. You asked the question and once the tears started to come it was only a matter of time before the words all spewed out too. As they did, I watched in horror as they hung suspended between us. For a second I hoped I could scoop them back up and swallow them whole before you realized what I had said.

In the midst of all this anger, this rage, this hurt and betrayal, all I can think of, God help me, is making love. To you. I want to take your face in my hands. I want to tear the clothes off your body. I want to feel the heat from your skin searing through mine until it imprints on my very soul, burning your love right into me. I want you to kiss my crying face. I want for you to taste my tears. Taste the saltiness of them, swallow them — so their sadness can permeate you the way it has me. So it can be a part of you too, the way it always has been a part of me. But you won't even let me touch you. I try and you jerk your hand away. I try again and this time you pull away with such force it sends me reeling. I know I should stop, back away, give you space. Time to adjust. Allow you to absorb the facts. Which are these: She is not who I thought she was. She, too, can lie. I am knocked off the pedestal, not worthy of your love. But I need to be close to you. I'm afraid if I give you too much space there will be no way to close the gap again. Now, for me, there will be consequences. I can accept this. The truth will set me free. Somehow it always does.

Each day folds into the next without things getting better. It's been two weeks now. I wonder if "for now" will turn into "forever." I thought that leaving was just something we'd talk about, fight about, and threaten. Not something we'd do. We'd never actually move, either of us. No one would really go. But here we are, ready to say our goodbyes. Although I doubt they'll be spoken because we really don't talk all that much anymore. We just look at each other with angry eyes. Betrayed, both of us, now that I have evened the score.

You haven't even asked me to stay. I told you I'm leaving. Put pain in your eyes. Found strength in my words. "I'm going," I say and this time I mean it. No empty threats. No nights alone with the kids at a hotel, where I'd tuck them into one double bed and then go cry in the bathtub until the water was cold.

Stand at the end of the bed where the kids all slept, arms entwined, hot puffs of air leaving one mouth and getting inhaled by a sibling. Sharing breath in a way that they refused to share toys. Wondering how I could manage on my own. Realizing I couldn't. Returning home the next day and setting you free of consequences, again. But this time it's different. I resisted the urge to run, I waited until the time was right, until I was sure. "I'm leaving," I tell you, and you don't even ask me to stay.

I stay. Just for now. There are things I must organize, first. In the meantime, I use my sexuality to try and seduce you. Find ways of being naked in front of you. Shave off all my pubic hair, hoping for a reaction.

It's all I have left, the only trick in my bag. But you don't even look at me anymore. At all. Funny how I am always reduced to the sum of my parts. Salaciousness is my altar. When you are sleeping and have let your guard down, I slide into your back and push my lips into the folds of your neck. Transmitting messages of love telepathically. Willing them into the base of your spine. Hoping they shoot right into your heart and find a home there. If I stay here like this, quiet and still, you usually don't move or wake, unless it's to relax into me, press your back against me. Perhaps you sigh in contentment, forgetful in your dream state. You used to sleep all wrapped up in my arms, our feet twisted together, tangled up in the sheets. Sometimes I'd wake up in the middle of the night to use the bathroom and you wouldn't let me go. I'd try to roll away from you and you would only hold me tighter. Now, you always come to bed after you think I am already asleep. And you always turn your back to me. Begging me to touch you. At least, I think you are. But I can never stay like that, just holding onto your back, not feeling your arms around me. I have to move closer. Touch you. Feel your skin. I fold my leg over top of yours and raise your shirt just enough to push my hand under it. So I can feel your warmth. Feel your skin. Touch you. My cold hand makes you wince. Awake now, you push me off, yank your shirt back down, and tuck it in the top of your pants. Then you hoist the blanket up around your neck and recoil deeper into your shell. You already sleep so close to the edge of the bed it seems impossible for you to find more space there, but you do. You align your body with the seams of the mattress, as far away from me as you can get. You get up a few hours later and leave for work. Think nothing of me. I wake up in the morning and eat you for breakfast.

I have the keys. I've paid first and last. I commit myself to at least two months away from you. I can't bring myself yet to think of longer. I am methodically planning what to take and what to leave - but it makes no difference. Everything I own was bought by you, bought with you, or bought with you in mind. I want to leave here to get away from you and all the memories here, but I guess I forgot how much of you would still be coming. I'm still walking in your shadow. I can feel you all through me, all around me. The forks I pack have all been in your mouth. The towels have been rubbed all over your body. My pajamas have snuggled up to you. My underwear has been taken off by you. My sheets have been entwined between your legs.

And then there are the things I leave behind. I leave them with you, for you to remember. Like the couch we made love on, dozens of times. The kitchen table where you'd sit while I cooked breakfast, making all your favourite things. Like the shower we'd stand in together where you'd wash my hair, careful not to get soap in my eyes. And the bed. Our bed. All those nights we made love. Until my body was just as familiar to you as your own. Where we'd lay in the darkness just talking and planning our future. Where we'd take turns sleeping, the whole night in shifts, while a sick child fevered between us. Sometimes we'd have our backs turned in anger, but even then you were never far, and I was just an arm's reach away. But not this time.

I almost stumble down the steps. It's dark outside and I don't know where to put my feet. I unlock the door and I am inside. Inside my apartment. It's still empty. I paid rent a week ago and never came back, until today. Today's the day I take ownership of this place. Of my new life. I can't find the light switches.

I wonder how long it will take for this place to be familiar. To be home. It's a basement: I am moving into the womb of another family's home, to be re-birthed, to start again. The bathroom is painted red: the center of the womb. I rock my head against the floor. It hurts so much I start to cry. "Start" - as though I had actually stopped.

I see a package sitting above the fireplace. It's from a friend - my best friend. The only one who has been inside my pain, who understands my loss. No one else even knows I am doing this. I haven't told a soul. Inside the package is a book. "You Can Do Anything" is the title. I flip through the pages. A quote catches my eye. "Treat yourself with respect so that others will know how to treat you." Respect. Did you have that for me? I know now you didn't. And it's because I allowed you to treat me the way you did that you did it for so long. But not anymore, and not ever again. I catch my breath and some of the rawness fades. Some, but not all. That little package saved me. Gave me just enough push to continue. I unload the car that I packed myself. I haven't had to move by myself in a very long time. It's a lot of work. But I am determined. I bring in the boxes and set up my altar. Spiritually I am in a good place. My breathing slows. I might be okay. I might. I pray to each and every Goddess that I can think of for strength. Durga, the Divine Mother, riding in on a lion. Fierce. Tara, the Goddess of Compassion. I feel her in my tears, like the tear she was born in. Kali, with her hands full of heads, torn off. Full of destruction. Forcing a new start. A Goddess, in transition. Me. Yes, I pray for strength. I'm sure going to need a lot of it.

I wonder what you are doing now. This is your first night alone, away from me. You've spent the night without me before - there were times when we would fight and yell and I'd scream that I was leaving. I might even leave for a bit. But you always knew I'd be back. There were times that you would leave, sometimes for a week, or two weeks. You'd pretend to be strong, pretend you didn't care. But you always came back too. The pull of your heartstrings always brought you back to me, and mine always brought me back to you. This time though, I'm not so sure. I guess I stopped being sure of anything when I found out about her.

There have been many times when I suspected infidelity. When I considered the possibility that another woman may have shared her body with you, touching you in ways that brought you pleasure. Whispering in your ear - or worse, capturing your heart. You always used to brush away my doubts. You told me I was crazy so many times I almost believed it myself. I would look into your eyes, searching for the truth, and I was always satisfied with what I found there. I couldn't imagine you were capable of lies - not the man I married. Not the man who rocked my kids to sleep, who made me tea when I was sick, who said he loved me. No, not that man. Not you. I would tell that little voice of intuition to hush, quiet down. I would tuck my insecurities deep down inside and forget them for a while. Until the next time. The next time you stayed out too late, or didn't answer your phone when it rang while I was beside you. The next time you hesitated when you'd come home and I'd ask you where you'd been. I suppose because you didn't confess and I couldn't find proof, I had no choice but to stay quiet. Even though I knew the truth, deep in my gut. There are none so blind as those who refuse to see. But this time was different. You told me her name.

Well, even that in itself was nothing new. I knew the names of the others too. The ones you called friends. The ones you would swear up and down meant nothing to you. The ones who backed up your story if I happened to ask. But this time you told me her name and this time you admitted it: the two of you had sex.

And once I knew some, I had to know all. Otherwise, those unanswered questions would eat away at my soul, like a worm eats a rotten apple: digging straight through to the middle. I didn't want to know just the external details. I wanted to know all of it. All of it. Dive right into the middle. Where did you meet her? *At the gas station.* Where did it happen? *At her house when her roommate was out.* When did it happen? *Two years ago.* How long did it last? *Only about a month.* "Only?" A whole month? Did it feel good? Was she pretty? What color was her hair? What position did you fuck her in? How many times? Was she prettier than me? And the big question, the only one you didn't answer: Why? Because you couldn't answer that one. Couldn't look me in the eye and tell me why, after you had promised in front of God, our family, and our friends to love, honour, and cherish me, to remain faithful for all of our days, until death do us part, why you would choose to forget everything we had built for that one single moment of lust. Why? For that there were no answers. There never will be. Although I ask you. Again and again.

The kids are all asleep. I'm sitting here in the dark. I could turn on the lights, but there is nothing I want to see. I don't want to see the tiny kitchen sink; it isn't the round one with the goose-neck faucet that I picked out for our house. I don't want to see the blank walls; I can't bear to hang anything on them, because that would make this feel permanent and I'm not ready for that yet. I don't want to see the purple paint in the living room, because I know my real living room is red; I painted it red myself. And for sure, I don't want to see this mattress, tucked in the corner of some basement. Where I know I will wake up in the morning facing a wall, my arms empty, your face not in front of me.

My thoughts are incoherent. I can't make sense of this. It's surreal, this new reality. Will I regret this decision? Time will tell. For now, I will hurt someone to make myself feel better. That's just the way love goes. I am speaking up for myself. My healing is a work in progress. My love for you will cleanse me, washing away all the pain held deep within. Say nothing of my love for me - healing my whole self is a project too large. Healing our love is almost unthinkable. So I will start small: today I will love my big toe. I will hope this love will spread. Eventually it may take me beyond my physical self, into the world where we exist as two souls. Soulmates, our forever kind of love stretching beyond infinity. Only love.

I'm sorry if I hurt you. Sorry and not sorry at the same time. I've yet to find a way to let go of my desire to punish you. To see that it does not honour my soul. That my life is a mirror, reflecting back all of my decisions, the good and the bad. Telepathically, I will your presence. "Come," I whisper, my exhaled breath the only thing to take shape as your physical form never appears. I am as sure of our connection as I am that the sun will rise tomorrow. It's what I believe in.

Once the kids are sleeping it gets quiet. And when it's quiet I can't stop my thoughts. All I can think of is before. When we lived together as husband and wife. Remember our wedding day? I never felt more beautiful. It didn't matter what I wore or what we ate or where the ceremony took place. All that mattered was the way you looked at me. Time stopped all around us. Nothing else mattered. It was you. It was me. We became us. Your hands were on me all day. Sometimes on my back, sometimes in my hair, sometimes around my neck. You touched me all day. I never thought you'd let go. Never thought the day would come when I'd have to sleep alone.

Did you go to bed expecting to sleep? Will you sleep, or toss and turn, sleepless like me? I took one of your sweaters from the closet. Did you notice? I'm always cold and without your warm body next to me I might need this sweater to keep warm. Or I might just want it, because it smells like you, reminds me of you, brings me closer to you, now that we are so far apart.

Do you think it will get easier? That someday our love might just be a distant memory that we can look back on and smile? Or will it always hurt this deeply? I wonder where all the best parts of me will go if you aren't there to bring them out. Will you reach for me? Do you still sleep on your side? Or have you moved to mine, to fill the void? To erase the space my absence has left, to smell my shampoo on the pillow? Do you line up your body with the curves of the mattress, the curves my body has carved in the years we were together? Will you cry? Feel sad? Have emotions, finally, if there is no one there to see them? Do you miss me yet? I will never know. I won't be there to hear your answers. Wouldn't ask the questions anyway. If I did you wouldn't speak.

I thought you would catch me. I sit here and fall. But you don't speak. You say nothing at all.

I still remember the day I loved you the most. In eleven years we've shared many breathtaking moments. But this day sticks out: I was pregnant then too. This was a baby that would never come, though. I never prayed so hard for something to be undone and then cried so hard when the undoing started to happen. The praying stopped when the bleeding started. All that blood to wash away the baby, who left as if in silent agreement with me that the timing was wrong. Please don't stay, I begged, not yet. Stay in my heart for now and choose another time to be born. Because I knew I wanted a baby with you. Dozens, in fact. All as handsome as you. As kind as you. As perfect as you. Because back then I didn't know you had flaws; I wouldn't have believed you if you'd told me you had them.

I knew I wanted all those babies, just not now. I didn't want this baby now. But then, when all that wishing and fervent praying to anyone who would listen started the very process I was hoping for - when the blood came - I couldn't help but feel guilty. Suddenly I wished it wouldn't actually happen. I prayed it would stop. Of course, it was too late by then. Some things can't be undone. Be careful what you wish for. With the blood came the tears. And with the tears came you. You held my hand. You took care of everything, while Mother Nature took care of our little accident. Could everybody do this, I wondered? Cause a baby to leave their body, simply because they willed it to happen? The guilt was tremendous.

I had never really thought it out, giving the idea of having this baby a chance.

Maybe we would have been okay - I could have left school. It didn't matter that we were only together for four months. I knew I loved you. It was okay if you weren't sure. I loved you enough for both of us. We might have been alright. My mind spun all my thoughts in positive directions. It would have been just fine. It was me that ruined it, just like always. When I passed a blood clot that was no bigger than a grape, it was already so much more than that. It was already a baby in my eyes. A full-term, cuddly, sweet-smelling baby that I had made with you. And I had just wished it away, flushed it down the hospital toilet because I didn't want to touch it. What if I had a doctor put it in a jar and take it for tests? Would you discover that it had spontaneously aborted because its mother didn't know how to love it?

I sunk into a deep depression. My eyes were too heavy to open. I wanted to stay in bed. All the time. Forever. I refused the pain medication the doctor prescribed. I felt the pain was mine to bear. You crawled inside my head and felt my suffering, understood it. You fed me when I wouldn't eat. You brushed my hair when I let it mat. You dried the tears that wouldn't stop coming. I hated myself so much, and all you showed was love. You took care of me. You took care of everything. Mother Nature allowed my body to heal while you healed my wounded soul.

We did go on to have babies. Maybe not a dozen, but enough of them to feel like it some days. They are all as handsome, kind, and perfect as you - flaws and all.

Being a housewife used to make me happy. Can you imagine? I found pleasure in the mundane chores of day-to-day life. I used to like ironing your shirts. I would smile and hum softly in the mornings while I made your lunches. I'd tuck a love note into your bag. Kiss you goodbye. Pretend not to notice that you didn't even look at me and only mumbled your farewell. Somewhere between you putting on your shoes and walking out the front door, carrying the lunch I had just prepared with such love, I'd wait for a thank-you or some acknowledgment of my devotion. But there never was one, and gradually I got used to the silence. Then came to expect it.

I married a man so distant he was never here to ask questions. I laugh at how little he knows me. And where is he now, my husband, where did he go, each and every night? He would get away from me as fast as possible. Catch me if you can. I used to think if he left me I'd be sick - sick enough to die. Maybe I would. But maybe not.

I have a headache that doesn't hurt. I sit in child's pose. Utthita Bahlasana: my least favorite yoga posture. I hate how it makes me feel. Vulnerable. I try to relax, to breathe. I am the keeper of secrets. I taste a waxy film on my lips and I remember: lemon chapstick takes me back to a place before now. I remember swimming with my mother, and how she never got her hair wet. It's my turn to mother now. I wonder what it would be like to leave, without a backward glance. Walk outside and away from my sleeping children, into the night. Swallowed by darkness. It's easy to do. I have been running away, doing this my whole life. I am restless, but alone. Alone, because to know her is to know all of her. All of me. The best of me. There's not one good thing about me. Is it me, then? Am I the reason for his transgressions? Have I failed this man, my husband, our children? I'm not a good wife, not a good mother. I'm the best mother. That's what they say, but they don't know any differently. I used to blame him, wanted it to be his fault. But now I wonder: how much of this is me?

A bubble bath to wash away my sins. Can I tell you the first time he made love to me I started to cry? Before it was even over. The tears didn't wait. He said, go home. Fix your marriage. You will never love another man. He was including himself in that tally.

He always knew his place. "Fix my marriage." Didn't he know how hard I tried to do exactly that? I tried to breathe love into it. But some things can't be saved, no matter how much you try. Infidelity is a deal breaker.

But sometimes, a love won't let go either. Especially when there's magic.

You always rescue me. Who can I run to now if not you? Because this time instead of running to you, I'm going the other way. Catch me if you can. I'm already gone. Apology not accepted.

I go back to the memories. Ignore me and I disappear. *At the kitchen table I sit alone: this is my mother's favourite punishment. I hear them laughing, talking, discussing their days while I sit and eat in silence. I've always loved words. Perpendicular — my first one, and all the ones that followed strung together, in excitement, in sadness, in every emotion; available when no one else was there to make sense of my days.*

Grade five, I am ten. A diary. Red, leather-bound and perfect. I write, transforming all those words into line after beautiful line. I write about everything, I write about nothing. It's all beautiful to me. But when I am angry, I write that too, unabashed. I hate my brother, hate him. But I am careless; I leave the book where it can be found, and it is.

I'm in the bathtub upstairs. My exposed skin is too cold, but I can't fit it all under the water. I'm not allowed to waste that much. I like to wiggle my feet between the bubbles and I do. I rock my legs back and forth; swish swish. I don't notice at first that I'm not alone. Startled, I see them: my mother and stepfather. Staring, silently, holding my diary: angry faces. I freeze, frozen now - even the skin in the water goes cold, cold, cold and I shrink back into myself, wishing I had a washcloth or something to cover me. So exposed, more by the words than by my nakedness, I struggle to remember what I had written. What did they read?

My mother screams but I don't hear her. I am transfixed by the image of myself reflected back in the shiny mirror above the plug. Today it's upside down and I wonder if it always is. I can't remember because I am trying to think but my thoughts are clouded by the words my mother is throwing back at me. My own words. The diary was a trick to catch me doing something wrong. We don't say "I hate you" in this family, even if it's true. Ignore me and I disappear, but ignore them and they don't. Too bad.

I watch my reflection, no expression. Just staring back at me, a bobbing head, floating in the soapy water, almost gone now, just a head, that's all that remains. Where did my body go?

My stepfather gets into the tub; he's the hardest to ignore. The water rises higher until I am covered, but I don't feel warm, even though the water is warm. I am cold, so cold. Without a body and yet still - freezing. Frozen.

He blocks my reflection and I can't see the bobbing head anymore. I stare at his navel, feel his feet touch my legs, and try not to vomit. His hairy legs brush against mine as he sinks deeper, trying to make eye contact. But I refuse. I focus my gaze and think for a moment that if I try hard enough I can stare right through his belly button and find my image reflected back on the other side.

He pleads with me to explain myself. Why do you hate your brother? How could you say that? Why? But my love of words is tightly gripped, bound in red leather, in my mother's hands, and I cannot think of a single word to say to him.

I still kept a diary after that. I wrote beautiful words about how much I loved my family, loved them all, especially my brother. The real thoughts stayed inside until they festered, begging to come out. When I was alone I'd let them, filling page after page with disgust and rage. But I'd never leave a trace of them anywhere. I'd shred those filled-up sheets into tiny squares and flush them down the toilet. Flushing, flushing, flushing, until every piece of evidence that I existed was gone.

During our relationship I kept a diary too. Filled it with beautiful words about how much I loved my family, especially you. Leaving the book where it could be found. But you never read it. Even though I wanted you to. Later, when I stopped writing beautiful words and let the poison spew, you still didn't read my words. Ignore me and I disappear.

It's been a week. My apartment still doesn't feel like home. Because home is where the heart is, and my heart's not here. I get up at night and pace. I look out the window and watch the moon. The black moon, the dark moon. Anima. The part of me that refuses to see what is inside, to look at how my fears have manifested as this reality. I wonder if in some parallel universe there is another version of me. One still at home with you, choosing instead to turn a blind eye, staunchly refusing to do the work and reveal the secrets of the subconscious. Out, Lilith! She is the only one still awake. Everyone else is sleeping - except maybe for you. The whole world is hushed. I stand by the door and wait for you to come through it, knowing that you can't because you don't even know where I am. I could walk to you. I'm so close and so far all at the same time. Frozen and melting too. Frozen in fear, so desperately afraid of life without you. Melting in softness each time I think of you. I really could walk. You are just down the street, around the corner. See? Even when I leave, I don't go far. Before I know it I have my arms in my jacket. I put shoes on my feet. I leave the kids sleeping and lock the door quietly. I walk so fast I am almost running. In less than ten minutes I reach the front door. Your door, now that I have my own. The car's in the driveway. I know you are inside. Home. Where my heart is. The TV in the bedroom is on. I can see the reflection through the window upstairs. Are you watching it, or is it watching you? Does it help make the empty house seem a bit more full, now that you are surrounded by silence? Now that the whirling-dervish children are wreaking havoc in someone else's home? Not our home, but another home. Because what was ours has now become yours and mine. Separate. I fumble for my key. Have you changed the locks yet? You told me you might. No, the key fits, although it takes me a second to open the door. My fingers are shaking. I realize that I forgot to brush my teeth. Maybe should have put makeup on. I remember when we first started dating how I'd get up early, long before you rose, to put on makeup, brush my teeth, and brush my hair, and then I'd lay back down on the pillow next to you. I'd watch you without moving, trying to match my breath with yours, until you woke up. You'd see me beautiful and think that was how I woke up naturally. Back then I wanted everything for us to be effortless, so you'd want to stay. And it worked - because you did stay, and for a while it was effortless. But then things got worse and didn't get better. And before you knew it, we ended up like this. Me, running out in the middle of the night, wearing only my nightie and a thin jacket, while our kids slept in a house that wasn't ours, trying to find out if you are able to sleep without me. Wanting, I suppose, confirmation that at least you were alone. So I run up the stairs, taking two at a time. The bedroom door is locked. I knock. Bang, bang, bang. It echoes in the night. Then you stand before me. You were awake, I can tell. I push you over, falling onto the bed. Our arms are all intertwined with each other's. I kiss you hard, full on the lips. You kiss me back, hesitant at first, then wild with desire. I peel back the layers of your clothes. Since when did you sleep in clothes? You undress me too, until we are naked and soft in each other's arms. I know every inch of you. I know all of your smells and tastes. I bury my face in your neck. You turn me over and kiss the small of my back. It's my favorite spot. But I don't have to tell you that. You make love to me and I feel it everywhere. My body belongs to you. You are my destiny. I want to say something. Tell you I love you. Something. But I'm afraid if I speak you will disappear, so I stay quiet. When it's over, instead of falling asleep in your arms and waking up there the next morning, I put my nightie and jacket on and get ready to go back to my own place. You look at me. I see it in your eyes. They say, please take your pain and leave. Out loud, though, you say nothing. What else can be said? I say goodbye and then wish that I hadn't. Because just like I thought, it makes you disappear. The walk home takes me longer. At least twice as long because each time I take a step forward, I have to look back - to see if you are watching (you aren't), to see if you will follow me (you don't), to see if you are at least still there. But mostly I look back because that's the real direction in which I want to go. Because once you go forward you can never go back.

I daydream this fantasy over and over. Wonder what it will be like if I do actually come to you, one night, after everyone else is sleeping. I can't bring myself to actually do it, though. I'm afraid of what - or rather who - I'd find in my bed now that I've left it empty. Left you empty. Instead I hope there is in fact another me, in a Universe next to this one where everything turns out just fine, exactly as it's meant to, and that one day I will meet her. One day I could be her.

I can't sleep. This house makes noises that are unfamiliar. The furnace makes a whistling sound. If you listen closely, it sounds like cheering. Like there are dozens of tiny little souls in the Universe cheering me on. I know that even if I do manage to drift off into a restless sleep, I will wake up at 3:33 a.m. On the dot. To the minute. In numerology, that signifies a cosmic yes! from the Universe. As if someone thinks this is the right decision, even if I'm not sure. If we were at a baseball field, I would be throwing pitch after perfect pitch, striking out all the hitters on the other team. But we're not, so I wonder why they are cheering. The only one to strike out in this game was me. There are no other players on my team.

In my dreams, I see she has left you a text message. I read it on your phone. You are a good father - you deserve to have some time to yourself after the kids have gone to bed. But how could she know what kind of father you are? I know. I know you are a good father, a great father. The very best father I could ever hope to have for my children. But how does she know that? I can read between the lines. After the kids go to bed, she wants you to come to her. And you did - you do. In my dreams, it's not past tense. I get the feeling that the two of you are far closer than you have admitted to me. I remember not too long ago when I paused to think of who you were texting those nights you were with me, laying but not sleeping next to me. Who distracted your attentions and diverted them from me? Who? A seed was planted. A story unfolded. My thoughts turned poisonous. Maybe it was you I needed to worry about. The perception of your secrets. The life I'm not a part of. At all. No matter how hard my ego tries, what kind of perfect it promises, none of this matters to you. But for me, those thoughts simmered, repressed, just got louder, like a sliver, just under my skin, they refused to be silenced. Though I tried in vain for gratitude it got stuck somewhere between need and the perception of loss and lack. If I knew the truth about the two of you, perhaps I wouldn't even try to save us. Would walk away gladly and never look back.

I always thought it was worse that you didn't love her. How could you, I wonder, throw away all that we shared for casual sex? In my mind, I kind of hoped you loved her, just a bit, because then it might make sense. As if it could ever make sense. Now I know: if you loved her, it would be worse. Far worse.

There is a knock at the door. It starts quietly. I can almost ignore it. Almost. But when I try not to listen it gets louder. I know who or rather what it is. I clean the bathroom, wash the sink, drain the tub and pick up the toys. But it's still there. I clean the kitchen. Empty the dishwasher and start again. Fill both the top and bottom racks. Wipe the counters. Clean the crumbs from behind the toaster. Still, the knocking persists. Why doesn't it stop? Go away. I sweep the steps. Mop the floors. I try and try to wash away the mess inside my mind by cleaning what I can. "If your house doesn't make sense, nothing does": my favorite quote. It's useless, I know, to clean externally in attempt to cleanse the internal chaos. It's very cluttered in here, both the inside and the out. So I try to make it go away, but it doesn't. There is no way to wash it down the drain. You can sweep some of it under the carpet, hide it in a corner, carry it out with the trash. It will never disappear.

When it gets too loud to ignore, I open the door to let it seep in. Your love washing over me, my anger towards you chasing it away. I thought for sure it was my past. Our past. Thought that was what I heard knocking, but I was wrong. This time it's my future - our future. It knocked and I answered. Now I have to entertain it, make it tea, nurse it like a sick child. Explain patiently why it has to stop coming, stop knocking. Tell it that it doesn't exist anymore. I had to choose: it or me, you or me, and this time, I choose me.

But first, you have to listen, nod your head, allow it to speak. It's only when you have heard what it has to say that you can politely close the door. Because how can you start off being indifferent, when you don't even know what it has brought you, what message it might carry? So I'll do that: I'll start by listening, then I'll ask my future to go, and to take you with it. It shows me a picture first. Of us, on our wedding anniversary. Oh God. I forgot. It's in three days. In three days it will be seven years since we took our vows. Promised our lives to each other. Before the seven year itch. We were not anticipating that this was what our future held. I wonder if it knocked back then too? Maybe it did and I was too busy to notice. Too busy choosing colors, buying flowers, and fussing over my dress to hear. I wonder if it would have fast-forwarded to this moment back then, if I'd answered.

I face the future. And the possibility that it doesn't include you. This anniversary would have been our seventh, but what about our twenty seventh? What would that have looked like? Twenty seven years from now will I pause on that day? Will I remember the youthful pride that carried us down the aisle towards each other? Will I remember the first and second and third anniversaries, and all of them up until the seventh, our last, reflecting on the happiness we both felt? After the seventh, what does it look like?

I choose to imagine our twenty-seventh as if we stay married. Our love strong enough to carry us through this crisis. I'm older and wiser. You are too. This moment that seems so important right now is long ago over. In this moment the present creates a past and becomes a future. Twenty years on, the pain I feel now almost doesn't exist anymore. It has faded into the past. It has been woven into the tapestry of us - a tiny flaw in the quilt of our love. Barely noticeable now that there are twenty more years of memories stitched into it. Twenty years in which our love grew in leaps and bounds. Who celebrates with us, I wonder? Maybe there are grandchildren now. Maybe our own children are facing the challenges of adult love, going through the same struggles we did. Perhaps they've learned from us and the mistakes we made, our love lessons helping them choose their own paths. Maybe they pause when fighting with their partners to remember the times we separated. Remember how sad Mommy was and how strong Daddy pretended to be? The joy we all felt when we finally reunited. Do they think back twenty years, to now? Do they remember the seventh anniversary, the one we spent apart, without each other? Or, are they focused on the present time - the twenty-seventh? The one we reached because our love was strong enough not to let go? I can almost see it. Taste the sweetness of the cake, which pales in comparison to the sweetness of our love. Feel your lips on mine, aware of your touch and how over the years it has grown familiar. We have reached a good place. My beloved. Happy Anniversary. Seven years now. Twenty-seven someday. Because I'll never let go.

I came home today to an empty house. My little butterflies, my babies, are all with you. This is still very new. Very raw. It hurts way down in a deep place. It's not even you that I miss, exactly, and maybe it's not even them, specifically, either. It's all of us together. We used to be family. What does that look like now, when I am here sleeping alone? The kids are in their old beds, in a place they still call home. What would it be like if it was only me? Motherhood, with its perceived and complete lack of individuality feels suddenly vacant. An unoccupied space, very much like this apartment. I feel the emptiness. It's vast. Stretching out beyond me straight into the Universe. The uni verse. The one verse. Infinite. I don't want to know. Don't want to be this alone. Wonder what it could be like to be alone but not lonely. I resist the urge to call you. Though perhaps I could get away with it tonight. I could pretend that I am calling about them. Pretend it has nothing to do with you, even though it has everything to do with you. It's the saddest thing in the world, coming home to see all the empty little beds, especially when they have yelled and screamed out their frustration. I take the brunt of it, of course I do.

You aren't here to see them cry and kick and scream. You aren't here when they yell "I hate you, Mommy!" You aren't here to calm their fears and feed them make-believe. It's only me. It always is. Though sometimes I yell "I can't do this! Don't want to! Maybe, just maybe, I will run away from it all!" I say this and flinch. They stare at me, wide-eyed, in surprise, bewildered by my admissions. Why am I the one to clean up yet again from another of your mistakes? It's so easy for you. Has losing me taught you anything? Does it sting like this when you come home and find your house empty like mine is now? Do you stand over their beds and wish it wasn't so, like I do now? Do you cry as I do? Sorry for them, for me, for you?

I didn't know it would be so hard not to take care of you. At dinner time I still think I should be in the kitchen, cooking. Not preparing tacos or whatever food the kids like, but slipping in your favorites here and there too. To keep you satisfied. Now there are only five places, not six, at the table. Less dishes. Less laundry. Less work overall. But I miss it, I confess. When I go shopping for food I might still pick things up that nobody except you eats. Will that ever fade, my desire to please you? I want to take care of you. Can you make it on your own? Who will fill you up if it's not me? How will you survive if I'm not there for you? I have been focused on inner strength, doing what I need for myself. It occurs to me now that you might not have enough of your own. Will you be okay? It must be worse for you. At your place, there's only a setting for one.

I wish I could read your mind. Peer into the depths of your soul. Climb right in, through the sticky black paste and see you. Know you. Finally know for sure if you really do love me. Would I be swimming around, awash in your love? Or is there nothing? A vacant hole, another lie, your love an illusion? Would I have to dig past the many, many layers of you to find it, or is it close to the surface, just under your skin, the way you are under mine? It's like those nesting dolls - Matryoshkas. Each tiny doll tucked neatly into one that is slightly larger. We are all built of layers. When you think you know someone, look inside - lift another layer. There's more. There's always more. It's up to you to decide how far you want to go. Will I ever find you? Bake you a chocolate cake to celebrate a love finally found? How can I, when my own mind is still a mystery wrapped in an enigma?

I get a phone message from him, just when I think he has left me too. There's annoyance in his voice - it's slight, but it's there. He wants to know why I haven't called, why I don't return his calls. Where am I hiding? I'm not hiding from him, not exactly. I'm hiding from the world and he just happens to be in it. I pick up the phone to call him. I hesitate. He already thought I was a lot to take. How about now? Now that I am lonely, broken, empty? Will he still want me now? Strangely, he seems to, if his message means anything. I have never been satisfied with casual encounters and wonder how long we will keep up this dance. Him trying to sleep with me; me trying to make him love me. So I don't call, but I send a message. Forgive me for being distant. I am just busy with the move. Trying to adjust to change. I don't want to overwhelm you. I know you don't do well with neediness. I think of you often though. I send the message to make sure he stays. This time I know it won't be effortless. How much can I ask from him, when he has told me what he can give? It's never enough; I always want more. I'm not even sure I want him specifically, or if I just want to be needed by someone. I'm trying so desperately to prove I don't need you.

I didn't want to like him. Didn't expect him to have character or depth. I had a nice little box, carved out just for him. I called it a one-night stand and hoped to leave it at that. But I'm discovering that he's really quite interesting, that I like him more than I thought, and much more than I planned to. I try to keep him in the box, to stuff him in. But pieces of him keep falling out until there are pieces of him everywhere. Now that Pandora's box has been opened, what will I find inside, wrapped in passive submission?

He drinks my milk. Each sip heals his mother wound, which seems, as far as I can see, to run very deep. I watch him swallow but I pretend not to notice. So it's never awkward. We share this intimacy. My lactating breasts let down a full supply as he sips and then gulps to catch the flow. This we can share, but it's never discussed. I'm not sure what the conversation would sound like, but I imagine it would be strange. I want to ask him if it tastes like what I had for lunch. Is it creamy? Does it quench the thirst I know he has? I want to know if he planned for this moment or found it a sweet surprise. Has he done this before? I remember my surprise the first time I realized what he was doing. I must have looked shocked, sitting in the front seat of my car while he dipped his head under my sweater and started to swallow. But of course, he didn't notice my expression. He doesn't look at me either.

I dreamt of you last night. I stood in front of you with my shirt off, shoulders hunched in pain. You took my throbbing, painful breasts into your hands with such love. There were two lumps, representing two pieces of unfinished business I was and am still holding onto. Your physical body seemed to fade as you became only light. The pain of my body - unimaginable pain - lessened with your touch. Your longing was so deep, so unfulfilled, I felt it too. Yours was a sorrow so profound it made me breathless. I weep for you. But I wonder, now, awake, if it's possible for him to suck the pain right out of me. I can make it his problem and not yours, not mine.

Some come to hurt and others come to heal. I have to wonder why he has come into my life again. I will never ask him for more than he can give. But I am afraid that I will leave feeling worse than before I came. I need him to kiss me, tell me I'm beautiful. Promise me he won't walk away just yet. I need him to stay for a little while. So I don't have to be alone. Never alone.

I feel my eyes burn: the tears, familiar to me now, sit just behind my eyes. Waiting. I sit here frozen, wanting to come to you, but knowing that you don't belong to me anymore. I have set you free, though I'm still bound by your love. I touched your hand today when I saw you. You didn't react. Didn't grasp my fingers like you usually do. Didn't even look at me, though I expected you to. Didn't feel my body quiver with the heat of your hand. There was no spark, no nothing. Just emptiness and cold, like you don't exist beyond the outer shell of you. Where have you gone? When you leave me where do you go?

Sometimes I wish my anger would not only surface, but stay. I flip-flop between desire and disgust. Love and hate. Hate: an odd word that rolls off my tongue lately when we talk. I tell you I hate you, but in truth, I feel only love. Desperately, hopelessly, unbelievably, I'm in love with you. Take it back: I want to demand that you take it all back. Give me what's mine. The anger, you see, surfaces but never stays.

I have broken the golden rule. I have filled him to the point of my own emptiness, giving away much more than I can afford to lose. He can't handle my intensity, can't reciprocate it. I want him to at least make room for it, but he simply can't. It's just not in him to do so. I know this. But I push anyway. I am used to getting my way. He is the lover who fills me up but leaves me unfulfilled.

I used to listen when my kids talked. Sometimes I'd just listen to the things they would say to each other, to the things they would say to me. Just listen. And smile. Happy that they needed me, pleased with the voices that made our house a home. But I don't hear them anymore. I still smile and nod, but I don't hear the words. I don't hear what they are saying because my own thoughts have gotten loud, taken over, silenced everything else. Sometimes I have to clap my hands over my mouth so I don't say his name. I see his face everywhere and wonder why no one has noticed my sudden silence. Although, I suppose that has always been part of the problem. No one really notices me at all here. As I retreat into my own space, where only he and I exist, I imagine again the way he moves my body. Foreign. Never familiar. Never quite comfortable, like when I am with you. Different. Electrifying. He'd move me where he wanted me and I'd bend and flow. Dreamy. Like the state I remain in for days and days after I have seen him. An ethereal girl in an ethereal world.

I smell lilacs. The wall behind me pulses. I feel the energy contained within it. The felt experience is always the truth, yours or mine. I close my eyes to meditate. Stay focused on my breath. I feel the swirl start in my spine. It whirls up and around, taking its time. It rocks my body like a pendulum. Back and forth. A grandfather clock, grandmother's clock, chiming on the hour, hickory dickory dock. I start to sway so intensely it rocks me inside and out. I keel from side to side, nearly knocking my head on the floor each time - or at least that's what it feels like. I try to adjust and make subtle changes: I rock front to back instead, but it's no use. I can only continue rocking laterally, side to side. I hate to break my concentration, don't want to open my eyes, but the swaying gets so strong I really am worried that my head will hit the ground. So I open my eyes, I peek just a bit. My body isn't moving. Not on the outside, not one bit.

"I'm going to cry," I tell him. The first time I slept with him I couldn't wait to come back home. Like a child sleeping over at a friend's house for the very first time: usually there's a midnight phone call to a parent, some reassurance from the other end. Enough to help you sleep, enough to stop the tears, at least for a while. What would you have said if I had called you? If I'd come crying like a baby, confessing my mistake? Would you have comforted me? Convinced me it was okay to stay? Or would you have picked me up and brought me home when I told you I thought I was grown up enough to do this?

Usually quiet, he suddenly can't stop talking. He's trying to fill the spaces between us with something other than you. "I really am going to cry," I tell him. I felt it was fair to give advance notice before falling apart at the seams - and now finding a tissue has suddenly become the most important thing in the world. I like to twist Kleenex into tiny perfect little people. Sometimes, after a good cry, I'll have a whole family in front of me, and I won't even realize I did it. "Oh no, don't do that," he said. Like I had a choice. I tried to choke back the sobs and stood there with tears rolling silently down my cheeks. I tried to subdue it so he wouldn't have to deal with it. And all the while he didn't stop talking, couldn't stay quiet. If he did, I suppose he thought the silence would get too loud, and what was unspoken would have to be said out loud. I wished he could say "I love you," even if it was a lie.

What does a person do with their wedding photos once the marriage is over? No really, I'd like to know. Do they keep the frames and empty out the guts? Burn them in some crazy fire puja? Give them to their children? Or do they keep them in a box? That's what I do. I keep them under my bed, on your side, where it's empty now. Take them out on the nights when I miss you the most. Spread them all over my bed. Cry myself to sleep and wake up with one in my hand and one stuck to my cheek; I open my eyes to a picture of you smiling, gazing at me tenderly in a way that you haven't for years. Then I quietly pack them up and put them back under the bed until the next time - which might even be that night - when the lonely ache burns a hole right through my middle and I repeat the same ritual. Over and over. Because it's all I have left.

He said "I'm sorry." I've been waiting for years for some kind of apology and I finally get it - but it's from him, not from you. He doesn't even know what he is sorry for. He just knows that my loss is so profound, so deeply felt, it makes him sorry. He's sorry, and he did nothing. You, on the other hand, have never uttered those words to me. Couldn't bring yourself to acknowledge how severely you damaged me, my self-esteem, my view of the world, my trust in our marriage. You can't bear to own up to the part you played in my destruction. I don't like to admit you destroyed me, even though that's what it feels like - like I don't exist anymore. But I don't: I don't exist in the same way. I am forever changed. You can't undo this. I bet you weren't sorry. I bet you didn't cry.

I used to dream of dead babies when I was small. Dead babies under a Christmas tree, wrapped up like gifts. White sheets replace the paper; there are no bows. They're in front of a window so we all can see. A sacrifice of babies. In my dream my stepfather would tell me, "How lucky you are not to be a part of that family. The one with the dead babies." Sadistic, he would tell me this so our family would seem normal. So I would go home with my own parents and not want to leave, because look at the alternative.

Now I dream of water. A baby almost drowns. I save the baby and find comfort in the water, floating with the baby, until we fall down a waterslide. There are fish tanks and tiny Buddha's.

I tell a friend, a fellow yogini, how much I hate child's pose. It makes me feel vulnerable, weak, and afraid. "Really?" she asks. "I love child's pose. It's so nurturing. It feels warm and safe, like being inside my mother's womb," she says. I am jealous for a second. I never feel nurtured. I don't know what it feels like to be warm, because I'm always cold. Always. I don't know what it feels like to be safe. I thought I had found safety in you but my safe harbor didn't exist: I almost drowned. As for my mother, her womb must have been a hostile place. I have never felt loved by her. For a second, though, I miss her. I almost want her. But then I remember: she is just like the rest. She set the standard for every relationship I would ever have as an adult. And she set that bar very low. I decide I want to stay alone this time, until I can raise the bar for myself - until every relationship I have going forward is nurturing, warm, and safe. As I try to see child's pose in this new way, as a satisfying reflection of self-love and a way of creating protection from within, I wonder if I will ever be able to embrace it. Or will it always create for me the experience of being exposed, defenseless, helpless? Like I felt when I really was a child, when being weak and vulnerable was dangerous?

Curled fetal, I awaken. The dream is fresh, it haunts me: I am running up the stairs as I did in some distant childhood memory. My mother is in bed, as she was on that day too. Frantic, I shake her. "Where is the restaurant, the restaurant, where?" Through a door there is a shower stall. Little girls, pale faced and silent, stand in a line. They are naked. White makeup is smeared across their faces and their tiny, underdeveloped bodies. The music teacher, he has no shame. I attack. I am a powerful mother bear. He resists, but I fight harder. I am strong.

I wake up terrified. In bed I cry, still curled fetal, longing for comfort. But I am alone, and disoriented. It takes a moment for me to place myself as an adult, in my own room. Safe.

Eventually I decide I am not satisfied with the ending. For this dream, I want more. Closing my eyes, I go back. To the shower, to the girls, to face their abuser. This time I'm lucid, aware. I hold his arms behind his back. Force him to look at me. "If you even think about saying anything other than 'I'm sorry' to those girls (for they are my girls, my twin girls) I will cut your dick off and shove it in your mouth." He doesn't nod. He stays silent. I force him over to where my girls stand. They are still. Afraid. "I am sorry. I am sorry," he says and for a moment I believe he is sincere. They stare, wide-eyed and silent. Forcefully, fierce-fully, I say to them, "He is the one going to prison. Not you. You must not imprison yourself for a lifetime because of someone else's choices." I am empowered. Angry at what is unfolding, but adamant, absolutely adamant that those girls, those 10-year-old girls, not carry his shame or make it their own. When I awaken I am afraid, but also stronger. My inner child is healing.

I thought I was alone in the room, but in the corner I see him: there he is. Infidelity. Infidelity is sitting beside my good friend Depression. And over there, always close by, is Deception. Liar, liar, pants on fire.

My breath catches and I want to admonish them for coming here. Why here, why now? But of course, they belong here now. Infidelity chastises me softly. "Where else would we be? Once we've been invited into a marriage..." he trails off. It doesn't need to be said.

He keeps his distance from me emotionally. And I keep a physical space between us to protect my feelings. If he gave just a little I might let him touch me, hold me while I fall - while I fall in love with him. I like it when he shows me a softer side of himself, the one he keeps hidden from most of the world and shows me only in glimpses. He is vulnerable, but only for a second at a time. I want to kiss him very softly - one eyelid, then the next. Hold his face in my hands. Tell him that I love him. That I'm here, that I won't hurt him, like others have before. But of course, I cannot make such promises. For he does not belong to me, nor I to him. There wasn't much else to say. A flight risk and that is all. But the pain is delicious. The torment feels alive. Rejection is familiar. It tastes good in the back of my throat behind my tears. I am drowning in my mind's creation and wonder how I got here, again. The movement stops. I am stagnant, stuck. Fear is alive and it wheezes out of my mouth as I gasp, breathing in and out. In and out. Fast. Anxiety attacks? It's been years. But here they are.

I try to redirect his hands, suck in, pull back, adjust my jacket. My attempts are futile. He wants to touch my stomach, knead the flesh, feel the softness. I wonder why, with all the places he could touch me, does he always go back to the one that makes me the most uncomfortable. I watch him, looking for some reaction. Displeasure? Disgust? But I don't see either. For me, it's the ugliest place. For him, it's not. He just looks comfortable. My body has become familiar. "Why?" I ask him. "I like it," he answers, as if that is enough. But me, I always want more.

They say when you break up with someone, the time it takes to heal equals one month for each year you spent together. For us, it was eleven. So will it be eleven long months before I will feel whole, feel happy, stop crying, want to live again. But then, eleven months hardly seems long enough. It might not even be long enough to sort through and separate all of the photos. I always go back to the photos. I can't tear myself away from them. Photos of us holding hands, laughing, vacationing, smiling, celebrating. Living. Sharing. If I erase you from my life, what would it look like? Take away the times we spent together and what's left but nothing? It's that nothingness that consumes me. There are so many memories, I can't let go - but holding on is dangerous. So, I divide the photos and then when it's nighttime and the kids are sleeping and I am alone and lonely, when I reach for a book of memories because my memories of you are fading, when I pull the album into my lap so I can hope to remember, you won't be there. You will have vanished, disappeared. I will flip the pages and see them empty. It'll be almost as if you didn't exist at all. See? I can tell myself anything.

His birthday is coming up soon. I buy him a gift. It's a sweater, size XL. I realize too late that that's not his size, it's yours. He is smaller than you. He doesn't have the broad shoulders or the wide back that I could curve my body perfectly into. I wanted him to be my knight in shining armor, coming to rescue me from the pain in my heart. Aren't saviours supposed to be big and safe? Don't they have to fight and slay giants? I know what he was up against was huge - so why is he small? How come I didn't notice that before now?

Even an L would be too big - I bet he's an M. Could probably fit snugly into an S. You are XL. Sometimes double. I bet you could crush him with one of your arms. Do you ever want to? Smash his face? Break his legs? Make him suffer, just a bit, for taking me? Do you ever want to beat yourself up? Suffer, just a bit, for causing this?

I had to sit myself down for a serious reality check. I realized what I was doing: taking everything I had put into you and giving it to him. Even though he has told me time and time again that he doesn't want me, not in that way. That he isn't available to love me, not the way I want. I try to take care of him and he refuses. He only wants to give, never take. But what he offers isn't enough. He can only offer what he has and I know this, but still. Somewhere along the way it became important that he love me. This is a pattern, I realize, that repeats itself. I forgot to care about whether or not anyone is worthy of my love. It just became something to give away, a valueless commodity. I wonder if someone could ever give me the love I don't have for myself. I'm not interested in material gain; the finer things in life, for me, have always been found in simple pleasures. I want for little more than to share an ice cream cone, or sit in front of a fireplace with someone on a cold, wintry day. You knew this and gave me just enough to keep me coming back - but never enough to satisfy. It came in delicious little slices.

Now with him, my cup is filled, but not to overflowing. I still haven't found what I'm looking for. I know I am supposed to keep my feelings out of this, because who in their right mind would fall in love with someone who is supposed to be a one-night stand? But now I see it is inevitable. It's no longer a question of if, but when. When will my growing feelings fully consume me, turn to love? It won't be reciprocated, and I tell myself I am prepared for the moment when he discovers that I love him and I discover that he does not. But I can't imagine him not loving me back. Can't imagine that in the spaces where he fills me that he will have only emptiness. Always so hopeful, I trail behind him, observing the changing seasons, marveling at the waves and how they pattern as they dance to the shore. But I am not there with him. Not present. Words fall out of my mouth before thinking and in that second we both realize I am gone. Have you ever been somewhere and wanted with all your might to be somewhere else? Even if - and almost especially if - where you are is full of beauty and potential? Do you find that the more perfect the moment is, the more difficult it is to be there? To just sit with it, believe you deserve it? It's self-sabotage at its finest. When did you start to believe so much in the lies that they became your truth?

I dream of you. We drive to a body shop. A saleswoman explains a new product. Car shampoo. I listen. I sit beside you on the couch, reading a newspaper. The saleswoman is her. She talks about your son, the one you share with her. I pretend not to listen as you talk. I read my paper. She laughs now at how much money I will spend - her commission for a big sale. I pick up a basket and gather products from all over the store. Faster and faster, I fill the basket until it's overflowing. She goes to the cash register to ring up my sale. I take the basket and dump it over her head. Bitch.

I need to purge myself of you. Your energy is so negative it depletes me every time. Your soul so needy it drains me, leaves me empty when before I was whole. I watch in horror as the numbers on the scale creep back up. I'm trying to fill the need you create in me. For even as I've wanted to fill you, I am trying to close the gaps in my own self by filling them with food. What am I hungry for? This is a deep craving for love and acceptance. If you care, then I will too. But it must stop here: this is not the legacy I want to leave my daughters. I want to show them self-control. Keep your hands out of the cookie jar. Never over-indulge. Look what happened to us! You carved a hole in what used to be me, you scraped out my insides like a pumpkin at Halloween. Tiny daggers shoved through my heart. The seeds of my soul all fed to her, toasted and warm, her body open and receiving while I lay carved into a grotesque form, smiling an eerie, artificial grin, watching everyone around me recoil in horror. I'm a skeleton of what I used to be. Discarded at the end of it all. You have a new bag of treats to please your mouth into silence, your craving satisfied.

I am ignored. I don't have to pass away and reincarnate. I have been born and reborn into the same sorrow and pain in this very lifetime. Little pieces of me surrender each time you break my heart. If glass is made from sand, then I am a thousand tiny grains waiting to be molded, shaped by you. Both of us are made of glass - but somehow you manage to jump straight into the fire and emerge unscathed. You melt, bend, twist, reshape. Poker-hot. Intact. I retreat into the coldness and the darkness and splatter like tiny drops of blood. I splinter into microscopic bits. I must stop seeking your warmth and find the heat within myself.

I'm bound by primal duty. In secret I seek freedom from this sad existence where my only life is one of lies. Where true happiness doesn't exist. It appears to come in little slivers, but, when revealed, are but reflections of happiness: broken glass, tiny shards of crushed mirror, imaging a broken me. The duty, of course, is to fulfill the obligations - to family, to the one we created, nurture, and love. Without us, they cease to exist. Our reality changes theirs.

It's frustrating to be alone with the kids. I forgot that leaving you meant taking them - it means being alone but without the benefit of solitude. I want you, and so do they. Unable to verbalize their newly-felt pain they react by disobeying in whatever capacity they can. "I'm not bad," she says. My small daughter, now sorry for another day gone wrong. "I'm not bad." Not bad. I tell her she's not bad, her behaviour is bad. But I love her, I love her, I love all of them. She tells me I'm stupid. Stupid, stupid, stupid Mommy. I think she's right. I say it to myself too.

I wake and sleep. Sleep and wake. I dream of my mother. We are at the beach. A wave comes and knocks her down. I am surprised to see her swim. She never gets her hair wet. I laugh as she emerges. "You have never swum in the ocean, have you?" I ask. I walk waist deep into the water, stay slightly behind her. She dives under the water in a somersault. I gently push her back to the surface each time.

My dreams continue. This time, it's you. I enter an elevator and push the number 16. It's the floor you lived on, one of the times you left me. I think I must have been looking for you, wanting to visit. The elevator is shaped like a letter D. I wait for the elevator to reach the top. I tip my head back and watch it climb the cables. Suddenly it flips over and I fall. Head first. Down, down, down. Just before I am about to land - all I can think of is dying - I separate, pull away from my body. My body crashes to the hard floor below. You are there, rushing to my broken but empty body. You hold it and cry. I hover slightly above the empty shell that used to be me. I sit with my legs in lotus. I want to tell you, "Look, I'm not dead. I still exist. I'm here." But you mourn the loss of my body and do not see my spirit.

The last illusion: you. I search everywhere and find nothing. I'm fairly certain now you never existed at all. Should I let go of my plans for you? Sometimes, I confess, my dreams of you and my dreams for you are undistinguishable in their sameness. Are you real at all or just a temporary manifestation born of need into my reality? Temporal, as all illusions are? How convincing your presence! I continue to look for perceptible memories, something to hold. But there is nothing. Not even a clear picture of what I think should be there. Tricks of the mind - fooled again, silly rabbit. You are only about as real as I think I am and perhaps that too should give me pause. Satisfied that I could at least make my Self appear at will, again, I come up with nothing. Though believe me, I have searched. What then, am I? Eternally seeking, the hidden and found. A cosmic game of nothing. Without my desire to give you form, where now have you gone? Dissolved into the tiny, flawless details created of my longing? A perfect, cosmic possibility. I wave my hand and you scatter in the sea, the soup of eternal potentiality.

I used to hide rent money, in case you left me, so I wouldn't get stuck. And you did leave, and I took you back every time and you always said "This time will be different". But do people really change? I tell myself over and over not to trust you.

I'm forgetting all kinds of simple things now. Like brushing my teeth. Sometimes I don't even remember to go to the bathroom. I'm ignoring all my body's signals, shutting down inside and now out. I took the mirror down in the washroom. I can't bear to look at myself. Don't want to see what's in my eyes. Don't want to look straight at the pain, don't want to see how scarred I am.

He isn't you. I wanted him to be you. Wanted him to fix the gaping hole that loving you has left inside of me. All of me: a hole. There's nothing left without you. And he isn't you, he can never be. Don't you see the truth? The fulfilment I have projected onto him? I wanted him to fix me. Wanted to give him all my broken parts and have him set them in some kind of reasonable order that I could look at and say, "Yes, this makes sense," and take them back. Own them again. I wanted so badly to forget you that I ran straight into the arms of someone, anyone, the first one to look at me and say things that didn't hurt me. I am forever searching outside of myself. I didn't realize I was taking over where you left off, and allowing the hurt to continue. Giving away broken pieces doesn't get them fixed. In his hands, they only crumbled further and then slipped through his fingers. Like sand from an hourglass. "Take my heart. Go on, take it." But he doesn't want it. You had it and didn't know what to do with it. It's the only one I've got. I'm supposed to be careful not to let it break. In a tiny featherless bird's chest you can see the heart beating right through the thinness of its skin. How to be so vulnerable, so exposed and raw. And yet alive. I should have thought of this earlier, before I gave it away. In truth, I didn't want it myself. I didn't quite know what to do with it either. But what if in a bold and somewhat desperate act I decided this time not to give it away? To pick it up from the dust and blow life into it again, to keep it? Own it, have it, take it out every once in a while. Hold it in my hand - tightly, ever so tightly, but gently too. Look at it, feel the pulse, see the scars: mine. Proof that I survived.

What is my lesson, hidden in the depths beyond the surface? Why does it keep coming back to me? Maybe I need to remember who I am, what I am, where I came from. Then and only then will I know again where I am going. Seems I've gotten lost along the way. But there might be hope. My internal navigation system always leads me back to you. But what if I take a different route this time? Perhaps my final destination will always be you. That might not change, but the way I get there might. An interesting idea and one worth exploration: that instead of rushing back, taking the shortest, fastest, quickest route, I take my time. I will find you, where ever you may go. But somewhere along the way, I must - I must - find me first.

I see him again. I have to. I just can't bear to be alone, not for one more second. I create drama to hinder my progress. He still doesn't look at me, still doesn't love me, but it doesn't matter. He holds me. He lets me cry. He pretends not to see my tears. He doesn't wipe them away like you would, doesn't let me sob into his neck, doesn't rub my head for me. Like you would. The problem is you were always the one to make me cry, and at least he doesn't do that. We don't speak much; he never has much to say. I talk enough for both of us - too much, perhaps. Letting out all my secret thoughts, the thoughts I have of you. It's never good to speak of an ex-lover in front of your new one, but he doesn't mind. It helps remind him that I am not his.

It still bothers me that he won't let me do things for him: I want to cook for him, take care of him, but he wants nothing. I don't know what to do each time he rejects my offers. With you, I did everything: I gave and gave, and I never had time to focus on me the way he wants me to. "Be alone," he says.

Our goodbyes are delicious. It's the sweetest part of our time together. I almost want to rush through. Hurry up. Get to the end. Each time we meet, I tell him it will be our last, but it never is. I have discovered, though, that when I tell him that, he opens up to me. Our conversations deepen. He looks at me, tells me I'm beautiful. He unwraps himself, choosing now, in what I have said will be our last moment, to reveal a little segment of himself that I wouldn't have been allowed to see otherwise. It's beautiful. He's beautiful. Our break-ups are so touching - even though we don't have a relationship. "We don't work," I tell him, as I stroke his hand. He looks at me, surprised. I have said this to him now many, many times. But each time feels like the first. He doesn't address it immediately. This is usually when he starts to talk really fast, not breathing in the gaps because there aren't any. I can't speak, can only sit back and listen, absorb this tiny slice of him. Enjoy my silence: his gift to me. When he pauses, out of breath and suddenly exposed, I am even more sure that this should be our last moment. Because I know it will never get better than this. It will never go deeper than where we are right now. I sigh. He looks at me, waiting. "Can I call you?" he might ask. "I think we should just leave it where it is," I would say. It's so perfect now. But still it gets better: he leans in to kiss me, pretty sure it's for the last time. He looks into my eyes, touches my lips so gently with his. He pauses, looks right at me. Connects. Then he leans back in and kisses me again, brushing a stray hair off my face, using his thumb to stroke my cheek. And then he's gone. He gets out of the car and walks away, but can't help but look back. He stands there watching me. I really wish I knew what he was thinking. I put on my seat belt, I stare back. I start to feel a little sad. Is this really it for us? I wonder, forgetting there really is no "us." He turns to walk away again, pauses one more time and then waves goodbye. Once I have this I can leave.

Sometimes he calls me moments after I drive away. For sure he will call me the next day too. I don't answer the phone. I watch the number of missed calls climb, hoping he will leave a message, knowing he won't. Then, for a while, there will be nothing. I'll just start to forget him - no, that's not true, but he thinks it is. And since he doesn't want me to forget him, he will call again. This is how it's gone so far. Each and every time.

I keep looking over my shoulder as if you may appear at the lake, knowing how much I love to be by the water. That's why I don't come here in the daytime, why I prefer to come at night, when it's dark and I can hide behind the solitude. One night when I come, I see a woman. We both stare at the same moon, lost in the same silence. She wears her pain on her face. It is so raw it must be new. It feels like I have made an intrusion on a very private moment. I am embarrassed for her, but she does not notice me. She lights a cigarette inside her car and rolls down the window once the smoke clouds her face. A short time later she gets out again to pace. Deeply lost in thought, she gazes at the blinking red light of the lighthouse, hypnotized by memories I cannot see. In my hand I hold a letter. I want her to have it, but am unsure of its delivery. My recipients have all been anonymous so far. Left in washrooms, on benches, and tucked on store shelves, I've never known if, when, or by whom a letter was received. But this letter, I am certain, it is meant for her to read. I stand beside her car, almost daring her to turn. But her focus is strong and she barely blinks. Her car window is still rolled down and quickly I place the folded letter on her seat. Instinctively she turns, but I am already gone. When she returns to her car I sit in mine and stare, waiting for the discovery, but she does not find it then. Blindly, she lights another cigarette and I wonder what she is watching inside of her mind, what captivates her so. I don't know who she is; I've never seen her here before. But I do not think it's at all accidental that we shared this moment tonight. Sometimes I wonder what she thought when she found the letter and if she knew it was from me. Or if she's yet discovered she is me.

After you leave for work in the mornings I still come back home. I go into the kitchen to see if there are any traces of you there. I smell you in my hair long after you have gone. I always say that, and it's true. If that was all there was I could dismiss the illusion of you, but there is more. I might pick up your tea mug and feel its warmth, hold it against my cheek, knowing that less than an hour ago it was against your face too. It proves you were there, if but for a moment. I usually wander upstairs then. The kids are at school so I can linger here for a bit, absorbing all the bits of you that get left behind when you leave. I might hold your toothbrush in my hand. Touch the wet towel hanging on the hook behind the bathroom door. I follow your morning routine backwards until I end up back in bed. In our bed. I might flop face-down right onto your pillow, breathing in the scent of you. Hugging the pillow close to me as if it really is you. Inhaling the microscopic bits of your skin that shed from your body, making your body part of mine once again. I wish some of your warmth would get left behind because the bed is always so cold, just like the one I sleep in now. Or, rather, the one I lay in now. I'm so tired when I get here I usually fall asleep soon after arriving. You still take all your clothes off when you get home and leave them on the floor: a habit of yours that used to make me crazy. Now I like it because it usually means there is a sweater within easy reach - one of your sweaters, one that smells like you. I put it on and drown in the size. It makes me feel tiny and safe. I sleep long and hard. I dream of you, and wake up alone. It makes me feel silly, waking up in your bed, wearing your sweater. Without you. I wish sometimes that you would come home and find me there. Your own little Goldilocks, caught with all your things. But she didn't belong in that house with the bears and I don't belong in this house with you. Everything here is too big or too small. There is no just right. Not anymore.

At home, I have to force myself to stay in my bed. It's like all the pieces of my body want to ignore what is in my head and just come straight back to you. I have to sit on my feet to keep them from running to you. I have to keep my hands busy, otherwise they will want to touch you. I have to bite my lips so they don't remember kissing you. The only part of me I don't have to worry about or watch over is my heart. Because that, I left with you.

I haven't heard from him in three days. It's been agony: waiting, hoping the phone will ring, checking the computer for messages. Why do I need his approval? Why do I want him to care so much? I need him to love me. It's selfish, I know. He says he doesn't want to hurt me; he thinks I'm fragile. He won't get too close to me so I can't get close to him. He does this because he cares about me. I found it strange at first, how closed, how distant, how far away from me he was. But I'm starting to understand: I'm not a very safe bet. He's right not to love me, not to get involved. He can run, run as fast as he can, but try and catch me? I'm already gone, back to you. I realize his three days and my three days are likely not the same. I have time to think of him and I do so until consumed -

whereas he might have work. He does have things, I'm sure, outside of me. I know he has a life. I just want to be in it. I close my eyes and reach out my hand to feel for him, but he's not there.

Depression is lapping softly at my heels, pulling me in. Suddenly I'm drowning. Memories are flashing before my eyes, tickling all of my senses. I'm sinking into nothingness, I've gone numb. The hollow pit of my stomach widens with emptiness until it spreads and consumes all of me whole. I'm shattered into pieces, scattered across the floor, buried under a carpet, forgotten.

I wish I had tattooed wings across my back and hair down to my ankles that my daughters would comb and braid while we shared secrets, bonding as women. It's nice to be needed. Do you need me? Not nearly half as much as I need you. Don't leave me. We've only just begun. But I married a flight risk and can't stay lost forever.

Some days before bed I hold my phone in my hand, ready to say "goodnight, I love you". And when I wake up it's always you I think of first, before anything else.

When my head is still foggy from mostly forgotten dreams there are days when I'll even reach for you, when I sometimes push my face into the pillow after he leaves, before all the warmth of him disappears, and pretend that it was you. It was actually a lie I told myself. Do you see there is no separation between my past and future tense? Like it is all happening now, in this very moment, where things can be okay and not okay all at once.

Some days I don't even remember how I got here. It's like waking up disoriented after falling asleep on the couch, where things are familiar but still somehow not quite right and it takes some time to recognize: oh yes, I've been here before.

On the third day, finally, there's a message. I can't read it, but I weep with relief. I see his name and I shake. Like that first time when he made love to me and my legs shook and quivered. I couldn't stand up, could only rest my face on his arm. Inside I was dancing: emptiness dancing. I gave my soul away. I will burn in hell for this, I thought. But at the time I didn't care. Think nothing of me. He raised me off the floor, where I lay in a heap. He wasn't there when I fell, but helped to pick me up. And this is what I think when I see his name: I can be more than I am. I don't need you anymore. At least, I don't think I do.

He comes to me at night now. I'm not even sure how. I just know that if I leave the door open I will wake up with him in my arms. He pushes his body into mine. It's warm, but at the same time I remain so cold. When I look into his eyes I see nothing. They are void of all emotions; his movements are so mechanical and yet I crave them. I beg for closeness. It never lasts long; his kisses are short little pecks. I know his heart isn't in this. There is passion but no emotion. I search for it everywhere. He leaves almost as soon as it's over - a hasty goodbye and then he's gone. I dress myself in him, layer after layer. When I close the door behind him I rush to the bed. I pull up the sheets and look, hoping he has left something for me - one of his hairs, maybe, or a piece of lint from his shirt. There's a wet spot on the bed, but that's from me. There are no traces of him anywhere. It's like he doesn't exist. When he goes he leaves nothing. Nothing at all. But he takes something with him, every time he goes.

I wonder if my finger will bend in half and break. I took my rings off today for good. A symbolic goodbye. My finger is indented, narrowed by the pressure. My finger has turned black and I read somewhere once it has to do with the quality of the gold. But I'm not buying it. Perhaps it has more to do with the quality of the relationship. Maybe when your heart turns black it can't help but leak out of you, right from the source. I can still see the two distinct indentations on my finger: one from the band itself, the other from my engagement ring. But that one actually came after the wedding, not before. You didn't even technically ask me to marry you, it was just discussed, almost decided. Over dinner, one night - and not a romantic one either. Weren't we at Wendy's, sharing nuggets? How did it become part of the conversation? We must have been talking about the babies. The ones I had growing in me. The ones I think you married me because of. I wonder how long it will take for my finger to get back to normal. Or will it always look like this? Maybe I shouldn't have taken them off. Like those women you see sometimes on National Geographic with those gold rings stacked around their neck. I can't remember if they are ever allowed to take them off. The rings, supposedly, end up supporting their heads and keeping it from falling off. Or is that just a myth? I can't recall. Does anything happen to make you lose your finger when you remove your wedding rings? Or is that just a myth too? Who knows for sure? I do know, however, that when you sleep with another man and you have your wedding ring on, neither man will ever look at you the same. And the way you look at yourself will have you wishing that along with your finger, your head would fall off. Then at least you wouldn't have to look in the mirror and see it all in your eyes.

I am in high school again, but I can't seem to find my desk. Where did all these people come from? I push past bodies. They are crowding around a screen. The teacher must have decided to show a movie today. The students are cheering, grunting, laughing, and I push closer to see what they see. Engaged, totally immersed in the images, at first no one notices me coming into the classroom. I drop my backpack on the desk. Loud, much louder than I intended. It echoes. The sea of bodies part and I see myself on the screen. What they are watching is an image of me. Their eyes widen as they make the connection. I am a classmate, there, in the same room as them, but also supersized, on screen, while scenes of my life flash stupidly, showing painful images of my past, forcing me to relive the monstrous details, one by each shocking one, in front of a captive audience. A lifetime of pain flashes by in images that project straight out of me from my chest and onto the screen. Still, they cheer, grunt, and laugh. I grasp opposite elbows trying to hold inside what continues to seep out. I am leaking poison. Everyone is facing me now, a room full of people taunting. And so I run. What else can I do? There is no choice. My backpack is forgotten. I run out the door and know that this is the last time I will walk into that classroom. This isn't kindergarten, with naps and cookies, security blankets and happy-ending fairy tales. This is my story unfolding. Even as I try to bury the truth deep inside, it will find a way to be told. Secrets are meant to be shared.

It takes a strong person to move out on their own - especially a woman with children - but people do it every day. It might not be easy; it certainly wasn't for me. I had to put beds together without any tools of my own. I had to buy food with my very own money. I had to pay rent and pay bills and do it all on time. But do you know what is really hard? Forgiveness, of course. Letting go not only of your mistakes, but of mine too. Both of us hurt, and both of us are trying. You are doing so well without me. You have to, of course, because I'm here watching. It's the same for me, I guess: I have to prove it to you. We are making it seem as though we really don't need each other. But are we really happy?

You sit in my living room after a visit with the kids. When they are asleep I ask you to draw a tarot card from the deck, to shuffle first. So you do. I want to know what you are thinking and since you don't always tell me I have gotten pretty good at reading your cards. Each time you draw from the deck I can peek into your heart. Even if it's only for a second before you shut me out again. You draw: the six of staves. A victorious woman. You think a woman has victory over you. That woman, of course, must be me. But look: I have lost everything I believed in. I've lost my happily-ever-after and all that came with it. I have lost you. So how, exactly, does that give me a victory? The woman smiles back from the card as if only she knows.

I still cry myself to sleep sometimes. Not often, anymore, but I still do it. On the really lonely nights, I call him. Just to hear a voice. Just to feel connected - to someone, to anyone. The last time I called a woman answered. Breathless. She hung up so fast after I said hello, nothing else got said. It shocked me for a second. There's someone else? Really? Really? Then: reality. Of course there's someone else. Of course. I kept waiting for him to call me back, to offer some explanation. She was his sister, his mother, an aunt. I prepared my response: he owed me nothing, there were no strings attached. "It's okay," I'd tell him. "You don't need to explain." I'd say this even though I desperately wanted an explanation. This was a nice little reality check, though. It helped me put him back in his place. He will never love me, so why do I want him to so badly? How much longer can I run from my pain? In the end, he didn't even call. He might still be explaining it to her who I was. She's nobody. She means nothing to me. She's just some girl that I know. It's you that I love. And he'd be right if he said that. To him I am nothing. To you I am the same.

The other day I lay with him. I felt like I needed to prove he was still mine somehow, after that call. It's always a little bit weird to be at his house. It's awkward at first, trying to match up our bodies in a way that is comfortable. It's strange to be in a bed and not in my car, or his. My head finds a place in the crook of his arm. I breathe into his neck. We rest like this for a moment, side by side. Then something happens, so subtle he might have missed it. Or I might have created it, just for myself. I had my eyes closed and he turned ever so slightly towards me until our foreheads met. I felt a shiver of emotion run through my body. In that moment I thought I could love him. Really love him, not just the feeling of love that sometimes gets confused with lust. As we inhaled and exhaled in sync, I felt my soul connect to his. It was a moment of intimacy unlike anything sexual we had ever shared. It only lasted for a second and then it was gone. I shifted my hip suggestively and he grabbed my waist with enough force that our movements became passionate. But that shift felt strange. It was almost as if we had crossed over to another level, one made sweeter still because I know I can't have him. We didn't make love that night. Instead we grew quiet, both of us, contemplating where to go now.

These are the lessons I have learned: that there can be sex with no love, love without sex. That you can fall in love with a complete stranger. That there can be love after loss, again and again. That a man can make love to your mind and it can be more intimate than any touch. That there are people who can change you forever and can do so without knowing how or why or even that they have at all. That intimacy can be built from a single moment of lust. That it's easier to be honest when you are uncommitted. That it's easier to walk away when you have invested nothing. That you can even walk away when you should stay, and you can hold on when you should let go. These are my lessons.

I wonder: if I change my name, will that be enough to change who I am? If I had a pretty name would I be able to think pretty thoughts, have a pretty life, be a pretty person? I spend all this time with just me, alone with my thoughts, the poison seeping out of me from time to time. I've been desperate for freedom. I have got to let go - just for a stunning moment. Everything begins incredibly full then deflates, back to reality. I can't fly like a bird. And you are just human.

Will you hold me tonight in your dreams? Do you still make love to me, only in memories? Do you still want me? I want you tonight, but not in my dreams. I want to make new memories. I want you to be in them. I toss and turn, feverish in my sleep. I am sick. There's no one to take care of me. It's okay. I'm okay. I must learn to be alone. But I wish I had someone to hand me the Tylenol. It's so very far away, in the kitchen cupboard. I can see it, but not reach it. You would bring it to me. I know you would. You'd bring it with water, you'd hold the glass and watch me swallow. You'd bring me an extra blanket while I shivered with chills, you'd check my temperature to make sure it was falling instead of rising to danger. Or wait, was that me? Taking care of you? Like I always did when you were sick? Where were you when I was sick? I can't remember if you were there or not, if you were ever really there when I needed you, or if I was always alone.

He thinks I give too much of me, and keep nothing for myself. He tells me often that I don't live in the real world. He wants me to be like everyone else. He doesn't understand one bit the way I think the world works. To me, what is given is never lost. It takes nothing away from me, in fact. A candle loses nothing by lighting another. In fact, it gives back, in unexpected ways. I give and give and it fills me up, fills my cup to overflowing. I share kindness, I share love. The energy comes from above. He stays empty, stationary, listless. He thinks the world is full of dismal darkness. For me, love is the only reality, but he can't see the beauty in the gift. It stays with him, it goes nowhere else. That's why he has to stay away, after seeing me just one time — because he gives nothing of himself and doesn't get anything back. I give so much I always leave with a lot. I am far too full of light to stay in the darkness for long. Even when I'm lost in my shadows.

I told him I loved him. It just came out. By mistake. Did I really say it out loud? I must have, because he disappeared. I haven't heard from him in days. I try calling but he never answers. I leave messages and I'm afraid they are starting to sound desperate. I didn't realize his absence would leave such a void. I just couldn't help myself. I want so desperately for him to be you, sometimes I can't tell the difference. If I close my eyes and pretend, I can almost make him you. Almost. I am good at make-believe. I pretended to be happy for years. It's almost the same thing now, isn't it? I'm growing tired of his distance, his unavailability. I wanted emotions, so I created some for myself - and look where that got me. My real fear is that I will have to deal with the pain of losing you. I have been so distracted for such a long time I almost forgot about what I had with you. It was almost easy: you leave, he slides in and takes over. Except of course, he isn't you, he could never really take over. And now that he's gone, I have to really see.

I have shocked him into silence. Boldly, I push him forward, out of his comfort zone. Forcing him to acknowledge the deeper parts that are hidden. Always hidden. It's only when I think I have broken him this time, that the cracks are big enough for me to get inside, I see that in fact he has already shut me out. I am exhausted. He leaves me breathless. I wonder if he will be back or if perhaps this time I pushed too far. But surely on some small scale there is need on his part too. Because he always comes back.

Something broke in me today. I thought I was going home, but I don't know where that is anymore, so I came to you. I ran so fast my feet didn't touch the ground. All I could think of was you. Coming to you, coming home, to be with you. I left my sleeping children and ran into the night - really did it this time, after planning it for weeks. Not sneaking in during the daylight hours when I knew you'd be gone, but coming in the darkness, hoping you'd be there. Before I rounded the corner to our street - your street - I knew. I knew you wouldn't be there. You couldn't even wait. I saw the driveway empty and that's when I fell apart. My hair matted in my tears. I couldn't see to put my key in the lock. My fingers smashed buttons trying to silence the alarm. All I could think of was you. I came for you, but you weren't there. I ran up to the bedroom. I thought somehow you might still be home. I even pulled up the blankets, looking. Looking for you. I ran to the kitchen. Checked all of the rooms. I didn't need to of course, because the car was gone. I found the phone in the bathroom and tried to call you. I tried, but you didn't answer. Just like before, just like always. Today I needed a best friend, a lover, my husband, you. I came for you. But you weren't there. I stood for a second trying to make sense of this new life. Surreal, my new reality. I see your sweater on the wall. I have nothing to put in my hands so I pick it up. It takes me back to a memory from before. From a time before you. Long ago.

My husband is making love to my body. He doesn't realize that after his first caress and soft kisses, I disappeared. To a place even he can't touch. Long before he entered my body, it was already an empty shell. I had risen, drifted, separated, until I was gone.

If I'm lucky, I go to a place where I can eat green apples. I sit in a field reading books on top of a wooden crate. Perhaps I am mildly aware of him knocking softly. Or, better still, I notice nothing. I hear only the birds, watch the sunset, feel its warmth, forgetting for a moment that I exist as a person. My body is numb.

On some days, I am not so lucky and I go back. Back to that first forced act of intercourse. I am sixteen again, as I was when my soulskin was ripped away. I wore bruises on the inside of my thighs for weeks, and there are others I will wear forever.

I don't remember him taking off my clothes. I don't know if he kissed me or touched me before ripping open the door I had purposely kept shut and emptying himself into my hollow cave. I don't know if he used a condom. I don't know if it was a struggle for him to slide into my tight, resisting flesh, which tore and bled. I don't know what was going through his mind as he penetrated deeper and deeper, each thrust pulling me farther and farther apart until I separated and became two halves of a wishbone.

The small piece of the wishbone, who didn't get her wish, felt everything. The fire spread between her legs and burnt through her middle. She felt the bruises as they formed. She felt the pain as her skin began to stretch and tear and bleed. She was the one who felt his skin underneath her fingernails. The one who cried for help that wouldn't come, but stood laughing outside her door. She was the one who kicked and crawled. Who pushed her legs up in what was misinterpreted as a welcoming arch of invitation. She was the half who bit his cheek when he tried to kiss her face, now wet with tears. She cried loudly for him to stop. She whispered "no".

The other half of the wishbone stared at the wall. Noted the date on the calendar for future reference and gazed at the pictures taped to her bedroom wall. With Carly and Carrie, outside of Carly's dad's restaurant. She, wearing jean shorts that made her thighs look surprisingly slim. At a restaurant, wearing a sombrero. A cake with a lit sparkler sits on the table in front of her. It is not her birthday. Brief snapshots of her life, frozen in time. She pauses, takes a snapshot of her current situation. Adds it to the inventory of her future and past. She worries about the blood on the sheets. She is mildly aware of the bed frame sliding across the floor. Finally, it has moved away from the wall and her forehead is no longer being rammed against it. Her pillows fall on the floor. Her teddy bear gazes at her with empty eyes.

The virgin is getting fucked. How lucky for her not to have been a part of it. It is the virgin, the one who can no longer look her in the eyes, the one who drags her out of bed for unbearably hot showers, the one who shoves handfuls of food down her throat and then chokes on vomit, the one who was absent - it is the virgin who will gather all of the pieces of her. She will gather the pieces that have been lost, stolen, or given away, and will learn to love each one of them. That is the price to pay.

You promised me make believe. And here I am, broken. He disappears into a crowd of high fives and I am left alone. I change the sheets on my bed, already forgetting as the tears fall. My underwear is soaked in blood. No one has come to rescue me and I hold that emptiness; I cradle it like a small child in my arms and let go of the girl that I was.

Later that night I lost my sweater. I ache for the emptiness that filled me with nothing. I move my bed back against the wall from the center of the room and pick up the sheets and blankets which are still on the floor. Then I push the bed to the other side of the room. I turn the dresser on its side, sit down on the edge of my bed, and view the room from this new perspective. My bedroom door is opened slowly. It is not my friend, but one of his friends who enters. He says, "It's my turn now. Lay down. Spread your legs. Let me fuck you next."

I don't think about my bleeding, broken body. I have no energy to fight before I have even recovered slightly. If he pushes me, however softly, I will fall like a feather and open like a flower. I can't stop the room from spinning. I know that he can take and take and I won't resist. I have nothing left inside of me, not even the anger to push him off. Instead I cry. And cry. And cry. He is startled into silence. I can't find my voice and while he thinks I am worried about the size of his cock or how much he can hurt me, I cry because I have just made my bed and to have sex again will mess the clean sheets. He stares at me while I fall into hysteria, crying about bed sheets, mindlessly fluffing and plumping the pillows. He doesn't know my private thoughts. I might tell him, but he doesn't ask. I thought he could save me, but he doesn't. He stands there with his arms outstretched, opens his mouth as if to speak, but he can't. He looks for something to put in his empty hand, picks up my sweater, and leaves without looking back.

Again, I return to loneliness and work myself into a cleaning frenzy. Later, I bathe in scalding water. All the memories fade and sink to the bottom of the tub.

I wish there was a shower. But there is not. Only a tub. And it's dirty, like the rest of the house. But that's okay, I am dirty too. I fill the tub with water so hot it steams. The mirror disappears. I am nothing. I feel nothing, I think nothing, I just sit, soaking. Trying to wash him off of me. There are bruises on the inside of my thighs: four fingerprint bruises on each leg. He rips my legs open with force and shoves himself in me, again and again. I line up my fingertips on each of the bruises and repeat the motion. Open. Shut. Open. I remember. I forget. Hot water rushes into the opening. I feel hollow. I feel nothing. Open. Shut. Rhythmic. Hypnotic. The water cools quickly and I replace it with water that is near boiling.

There is a man watching me. From a tiny crack in his bedroom which adjoins the only bathroom in the dilapidated farmhouse he stares. I rent a room upstairs. I haven't noticed him yet and won't for a few more weeks.

Blood trickles out of my vagina and turns pink in the water. I swirl my hand and it disappears. I disappear. My skin is red, blotchy, swollen, wrinkled. I empty the tub and start over: a ritual I will repeat many times over. The man who watches me masturbates quietly and goes to lay down. Every so often he gets up to see if I am still there, and I am.

Open. Shut.

I need a memory. Accidentally, on purpose. Something. One detail to carry. I think of before. I think of after. I can't remember during. Open. Shut.

And then it comes. The weight of him crushes my lungs. I inhale the steam but can't breathe and I can't escape. The weight of him. I am crushed. I can't breathe.

I retch and vomit. I vomit on myself in the tub, on the floor. Beside the toilet. In the toilet. Bits of food, bile, and blood. I feel dizzy. Hot. My skin is blotchy, red, swollen, wrinkled.

I vomit and vomit. When there is no food, bile, or blood, I retch. I gag. I feel dizzy. Hot. Exhausted, my stomach settles. It knows that what is inside can't be pushed out easily. I am empty. I am full.

I take wadded tissue, blot my eyes, wipe my mouth, drain the tub, and go upstairs.

I wear flannel pajamas and a pad between my legs to catch the blood that won't stop flowing.

My bed is unfamiliar now in its new place. I watch the moon. Her light washes over me. The wrath of Lilith, in a shadowy rage, is flooding the room. She is almost full. She bows to no one. She is widening her circle of wisdom. She is white and unchanged. I am red. I want her to be red. Why has everything else stayed the same? Why am I so different now? Unhinged, I spill out. Color floods the sky until she is soaked in my blood, waxing and waning with the circle of my emotions.

Out of habit, I recite my childhood prayers, whispered softly at bedtime for years.

Now I lay me down to sleep. I pray the Lord my soul to keep. If I die before I wake, I pray the Lord my soul to take. Thank you for this world so sweet. Thank you for the food we eat. Thank you Lord for everything. Oh thank you Lord for everything.

NowIlaymedowntosleepIpraytheLordmysoultokeepfori fIdiebeforeIwakeIpraytheLordmysoultotakethankyoufo

*rthisworldsosweetthankyouforthefoodweeatthankyouL
ordforeverythingthankyouLordforeverything. Fuck. My
soul to take.*

Take my soul.

Take my soul.

Take my soul.

Fuck.

Fuck.

Take my soul.

I leave to walk home. I take your sweater even though
I don't feel cold anymore. There's a heat, now: an
angry kind of heat. It burns my feet and travels up. I
try to name that emotion, but it isn't one I know too
well; it's a raging, burning, anger. You couldn't even
wait! You didn't even answer your phone. You made
me remember the night with the sweater and you
weren't even home - to comfort me, like you always
did before. I am being forced to go through this alone.

All by myself. Because I came to you, and you weren't there.

I've gone back to numb. I much prefer to feel nothing. Last night I couldn't sleep, could only toss and turn and think of you. But tonight? Tonight I will sleep like a baby. And not the dead babies in my old dreams, but like the tiny sleeping ones in the room next to mine. Because now I know: home is where the heart is, and my heart is inside each and every one of these tiny beings who wake and call me Mama. I am home, with or without you.

I'm dying inside and nobody knows it but me. There's a new moon cycle: I dedicate this one to finding my strength. I refuse to be fragile. Do not try to fix me, I am not broken.

Two doors. Tiny children. My happily-ever-afters resting, perhaps dreaming. I open the door, the right one first, and enter slowly. I turn on the light, but it's okay: nobody flinches. I need to see them. Twin beds, twin frames, twin girls: different, but the same. My girls, my growing-up-safe girls. I am jealous of their sleep-at-night habits. They sleep at night because they are safe; they sleep. I want to kiss them, lean in, feel their warm breath on my face. I watch their tiny eyelids fluttering with baby dreams. But I'm not quite sure if they are real; if I kiss them they might disappear. That's usually what happens when I love someone. So I stand back and watch them from a safe distance. Safe. I keep my arms folded so I don't touch them. I want to - I want to draw their tiny bodies close to my own beating heart and feel the rhythm of theirs. Want to know what an unbroken heart sounds like. Would it beat faster or slower than mine? I don't know. I won't know, because I don't touch them, since they might disappear. Leave me, like you did when I tried to listen to your heartbeat, tried to make your heart beat in time with mine. I used to match up my breathing with yours while we lay side by side, so our inhalations and exhalations were perfectly timed. Were they mine? Were you mine? I like to think so. Just for a while.

The second door brings me to my bed. I sleep fitfully and dream of you. You are moving to the United States. I have a new boyfriend and don't care about your absence. "I love you," my new boyfriend says. "I don't love you," I think to myself. I sit on the floor and pick up the phone. You answer. I have so much to say, but you can't talk now. She is in the room with you. "I can't talk now," you whisper, and then hang up. Wait. Wait. I love you. Love you and miss you so, so much. But the phone has gone dead in my hand. I smash my face to the floor and cry.

A second dream: you cheat. I know this one. I sit in the car listening to you tell me the details. It's what I suspected but could never face. Horrified by the truth, I run to the stairs. Dressed in yellow and black, a man in a tinted motorcycle helmet does a body wave down stairs. Inside our apartment renovations are taking place. More people will move in. Steel bars jut out from the walls. There is no space left for me.

I walk up the stairs and into the apartment you share with her. I am more alive in my dream state than I am when I'm actually awake. I watch her folding jeans. When you come home, I push you against the bathroom wall, and run my hands up and down your body. "Make love to me," I beg. I kiss you. I whisper softly, "Why don't you love me?" You say nothing. "Kiss me back, please don't leave me," I say. But it's too late now. You belong to her.

I think about the woman that I am. I think about the girl that I was. She still comes to me in my dreams. I get little snapshots of her - of me - searching for love in all the wrong places, wanting acceptance, hoping that someone, somewhere will keep her, will not ask her to leave or force her to go or show her over and over that she never belonged. She cries a lot, this girl. I want to take her in my arms and cradle her gently. She wants such simple things so badly. I know her deepest wish. She looks at me with hopeful eyes; she can barely see past where she is. She wishes she could be where I am now, but I'm not even sure if it exists. Am I real? Is she? Will she ever make it through to this time, the one she is stuck in still? I know by now what's coming, and that there is no way to avoid it. Worse still, I know that it will repeat. I'm in the future. She's in the past. Time warps until both exist in the exact same moment. It allows me to sit with her. There are times when she doesn't see me; she hurts too much to see past her pain. I feel so bad for her. There is so much more to come. I wish someone would step in and protect her. But what's done is already done.

I made it to 17. Barely. I swallowed four hundred aspirin in my aunt's kitchen while she washed dishes at the sink. Handful after handful washed down with lukewarm tap water. "Your chore this week is the upstairs bathroom," she said before retreating to her room, leaving me alone in the solitude of the kitchen. The empty bottle slid from my hand unnoticed as I waited to die. Wanted to die.

The ringing in my ears started first, but even the loud buzzing wasn't enough to drown out the inner dialogue. "Eat me, Alice. Eat me." And I obeyed.

What does one do, exactly, while waiting for the madness of life to end itself, snuffed like a candle, prematurely? I cleaned my room. I destroyed the evidence of a wasted life, carefully removing the long-handled red hairbrush from the bed, for example. It was the same brush my mother always had, but hers was blue. I wondered if it would give anyone pause when they cleaned out my room, discovering it after I was gone. Would they uncover the truth about me? That I used the handle, turned backwards, to rape myself, again, night after night? Desperate to feel something other than numb, recreating the pain I tried so hard to run from?

I looked around the clutter of my small room, suddenly embarrassed by what I saw. A tiny garbage pail beside the dresser, overfilled with empty boxes of laxatives and the wrapping paper from dozens of chocolate brownies. It was a nasty little habit I seemed powerless to overcome: each day after school buying a box of brownies and stealing a box of laxatives. I did my homework sitting on the toilet. I stayed there until I was clean. After all the years I spent with my fingers shoved down my throat trying unsuccessfully to empty the contents of an overstuffed stomach, alternated by days of intense exercise and brutal starvation, the discovery of Ex-lax was a pleasant surprise. It was a habit I clung to for many years, until I met Mihailah who taught me how to detach completely from a body that I hated in an entirely different way. But the evidence of it mocked me now.

In the corner, several pairs of jeans waited to be washed. I couldn't wear the popular Levi's red tab with my body type, but I could manage to look decent in a pair of Edwin's. The name itself screamed status at high school and of course, I bought them in every colour. Desperate to fit in somewhere.

In my school bag, there was a notebook filled with doodles of my name with Doctor in front and MD behind. I spent hours at the library, reading medical textbooks, planning a future that would never come because a year later I'd drop out of high school and that would be it.

Mihailah. I don't even remember how we met, but somehow she became part of my life. At 15 she lived alone — an indulgence I couldn't quite fathom. She knew how to order coffee, which we shared, often only one cup because that's all we could afford. Together, over impossibly tiny cups of espresso, we talked about life and how it would be better, someday. She shared her life with me in bits and pieces but mostly kept it to herself, living in some distant future she didn't quite believe in. I knew that her uncle paid her rent and that her family had more secrets than mine, but that was all. It was enough for us to become friends.

After being invisible all day at school I came alive in her apartment. Or rather, we did, both of us bursting at the seams with conversation and chatter. I spent hours in her living room, never finding it odd that she didn't show me her bedroom. It almost became possible to believe we were normal teenage girls. "Normal": whatever that was, I wasn't sure, but I had a glimmer of hope.

But then her uncle started spending more time with us. She was different in his presence, unmistakably quieter and dulled with an emotion I'd now recognize as fear. I'd raise my eyebrows quizzically whenever I noticed her visibly stiffen as he would brush her hair, a glint of possessiveness, just there under the surface, and unspoken like so many things. But she'd smooth over my concern with a smile, beautiful and thin, with hair so big and so blond it was impossible not to want to touch it, and for this I envied the ease with which he would stroke her. I suppose, too, that part of me even wanted to feel his hands in my hair. I ached for softness and a gentle touch. But he only eyed me with suspicion as if unconvinced of my trust or worthiness.

One day I arrived after school to find him pacing around her apartment. He would stare out the window, do a lap around the sparsely furnished living room. Back to the window. Look outside. Slide the curtain back. Pace again. Pause.

Mihailah sat unmoving, as if dazed. Her enlarged pupils, slowed movements, and delayed speech confirmed what I believed: she was drunk. But there was more. "Tonight, we try something different, girls." Do or don't, there is no try. He produced a coke can. I was about to decline, having never fancied carbonated beverages, but this can was already emptied and cut behind the mouthpiece. He folded tinfoil over the top to cover the gap and pricked tiny holes in it. Hands shaking, he opened a small plastic bag half full of tiny white rocks. With practised hands, Mihailah held the can while her Uncle crumbled some of the contents from the bag on to the foil. Using the lighter to heat the rocks she inhaled deeply from the mouth of the can and exhaled blue smoke. The sweetness of its smell, unrecognizable, filled the room and as I watched her smile softly I knew I wanted to feel - or rather not feel - just like that. I never asked what it was, I didn't care really. I didn't live in my body

*anymore, so what difference did it make? "Your turn,"
she breathed, handing me the can.*

*I fumbled, embarrassed by my incompetence. I kept
blowing the ash and rock off the can as I tried to
exhale first, preparing for the inhale, to expand my
lungs with freedom and bliss.*

*Her patience made me weepy. Finally, I got it right: I
timed the exhale and the inhale perfectly to the
lighting of the rocks, which burned in sync with my
lungs as they filled.*

And then.

*I wait for it to come, am about to be disappointed but,
oh my, it hits me. Hard. My heart beats faster,
impossibly fast, and I am aware of it jumping inside
my chest. I am screaming inside my own head, but
no, it is not a scream, not exactly, just a whirring, like
a train speeding down the track. Fast. Faster. In that
second I want to do everything - I am suddenly
capable, energetic, and motivated. My words rush out
of my mouth faster than I can catch them - but wait,
no, I am on a roller coaster and not speaking at all. I*

ride the wave, exuberant and free. For the first time in so long, free. Not guilty or fearful or numb. Suddenly I am vibrating, every part of me alive.

And then.

Then.

Nothing.

It starts and ends the same: teasing me with want. More, I want more. I wish there was a way to stretch it, to elongate the feeling and make it last just a bit, just a bit longer. It takes impossibly long for the can to make its way back to me. The can comes back but the feeling never stays long. Enough. Her Uncle is firm, says it only once and puts everything away. I walk home different. Blowing air, exhaling out of the corner of my mouth like I was taught. Practising for the next time. The next time...

After the ringing in my ears comes the dizziness. I am in my kitchen with the empty aspirin bottle; I feel off-balance and the room shrinks and expands in my periphery. This is a persistent state of uneasiness. I wonder what to do next as my body chokes and retches. I refuse to let the pills come up and swallow back the bile, finding it ironic that suddenly now my body knows how to vomit. What should have been a fresh start would now become the place of my undoing. My Aunt is in her room unaware. My cousin is probably skipping school, her life spectacularly messy and so average now compared to mine. Almost convinced this is going to be how it ends, I watch my short life decline — but unlike death by drowning, my past does not flash before my eyes. It's always with me. Never leaves.

Suddenly, I am terrified. Not of death or dying, no; for that I was ready. But: who will be the one to find me? See the red-handled hairbrush? Know my secrets, all of them? Who? Would anyone come at all? For all those unanswerable questions, I knew I could not in that moment die. I could not leave myself so exposed.

So I get on the city bus and take it to the hospital. Pay my fare, take a seat, and finally vomit all over my shirt. The kindness of strangers: someone hands me a napkin. I try to say thank you but the ringing in my ears is too loud for me. Did I say it? Did I whisper the words or scream and shout them out across the bus?

I do not know. Round white pills, still mostly intact but soaked in stomach acid, bounce off my lap and sit on the floor where everyone can see them. But I don't care. I settle into the seat, rest my forehead on the window. Close my eyes. Wait.

The next moment I have of awareness, I am drinking charcoal in a hospital bed, dressed in a blue gown. Faces fade in and out. Hands try to force a tube up into my nose, but it does not fit. "Drink me, Alice. Drink me." And I obey. Getting smaller and smaller, tiny enough to disappear completely from a world which has always been too large, I weep until my tears become a river and I float downstream, carried past memories deep in my subconscious mind, and for the next three days I am blissfully unaware. I leave my body to fight this battle alone and sleep.

My kidneys almost fail but come back. My hearing almost goes but doesn't. Almost: there is nothing I can do completely right. Everything is done halfway, even this. Someone is taking care of me, but who? I've travelled so far away to the other side it's time to come back and I do. "I don't think anyone has ever done their own laundry in the ICU before" a nurse tells me while I stand at the sink washing my puke-stained shirt. I hang it up to dry knowing no one will be coming with clean fresh clothes. It's been three days and no one knows or cares where I am.

"It's almost time to go home" she tells me cheerily as I slide my Edwins on under my hospital gown. The psychiatrist visited my room and asked me what happened to Mihailah. I think back to the last day I saw her, but I can't remember when it was — because you never know when the last day is going to come, so you don't commit to memory the events that make it up. Just as well. What did we do that day? I struggle to remember, but can't.

Even though I don't speak of myself, carefully censoring my past, I am revealing so much - but when the hour is up I walk away and leave the hospital. I promise to make a follow-up appointment. I know I won't keep it, but nobody cares.

A few days and then a week passed without Mihailah opening her door to let me in after school. Abandoned and lonely, I wondered where she was since she was always home, waiting. I circled the coffee shops and went back again, this time with a note to leave on her door. I was not the only one visiting that day.

Police are everywhere. They bang on her door and it echoes through the hallway. "Who are you?" they demand, and silently I hand them the note: Where are you, I miss you, are you ok? "School. I know her from school," I say and then I hear bits of conversation that change my reality. Not her Uncle. A prostitute. Sold for money. Sold for drugs. Not 15. Not her Uncle. A prostitute. Sold for money. Not her Uncle. Not 15. Not your friend. Not your friend. Not your friend. Not anymore.

I never saw her again. It's been years since I thought of her, years since I allowed myself to think back that far - to a time when, for a moment, I was almost happy. When I learned about the sex trade, I am reminded of his hands in her hair and I know for certain that if she wasn't 15, she was younger, not older. But I don't allow my thoughts to drift to her often. It still hurts too much.

I bow to you. I sit in Child's Pose, trying again to feel it as a nurturing, safe posture. But it makes me feel vulnerable, just like it always does. It hurts. It makes my stomach ache. I hate that my arms are splayed in front of me, like I really am bowing to you. I sit there longer. My muscles start to relax but it's involuntary. I clench them in fear. I'm afraid. But of what? I can barely hold the pose for three minutes. I rock myself back and forth on my forehead. I notice that my breathing is intensely labored. I am panting. My arms shake. I am frozen in fear. I must release the pose. Get out. Get to safety. I am practicing my five least favorite yoga postures. It's my Om work for the yoga teacher training course I am taking. I had no idea how emotional this would be. Next is eagle. The arms are easy; it's sitting with my toes under my feet that I can't bear. I try to hold on, just for a bit, but I can't. It's no use. My toes fold out from under me. I can't handle the magnitude of the pose. Have no way of making room for it. I slide into side plank. It makes my back hurt. I try the other side and give up. I don't even make the thirty-second mark with that pose. Four-limbed staff pose comes next. I can't get into it. At all. My back screams at me. I fall to the floor. Now the tears start to fall. I sob. I roll onto my back and then onto my side. I hug my knee. The other leg reaches out behind me. I'm a broken pigeon. I sob. I press my forehead and face into the floor. I wish I could melt right into it. I wish I could not be here in this moment, I wish I could be anywhere but here. Finally, frog pose, the last of my five. I push my knees apart. I'm still crying, but somewhere deep below it there is anger. I can't get to it. It stops at sadness: I want you, I want my husband. The one who comforts me when I have nightmares, who makes my pain fade with his touch. I'm not prepared for how much this hurts. It's only the first day of practice. Yesterday, I couldn't get past thinking about it, couldn't actually do it. I want you so bad. I need you. I need someone to hold me. Hold me. Please. Please save me. I sit in frog for about a minute. My legs split in two. I am split in half. I am a wishbone. Today is day one. I have so far to go.

The pain in my back gets so bad I can't move. Can't get up. Can't walk. The baby cries in his crib and I can do nothing. I have to pee but I can't even make it to the washroom. I have to call you; there is nobody else. You come right away. In trying to prove that I don't need you I discover that I do. Yes, I can leave, rent an apartment, pay my own bills, and sleep alone. Except I can't use the toilet; I need you to walk me there and pull down my pants. As you do so, I remember the last time you did this for me. It was after the birth of our last child. You walked me to the bathroom, washed away the lochia and gently put me back in bed. You did it then because of love. You do it now because of love. Is that still true, or are you here because of obligation? How can you still come when I have tried so hard to push you away? "I don't need you," I said, each and every time you asked. Except now I do. You take me to the doctor and feed me the pills he prescribed. Comatose, I lay in bed. I can do nothing more. Divine teacher, what is my lesson here? I try to be independent and end up needing you so much I literally cannot function without you. Now, my external world reflects what I feel inside. I spend a few days in a haze of morphine. I dream vividly, I find answers in my sleep. I wake and remember nothing. I notice that you don't look at me much anymore. I ask you to love me, now, just weeks after I've asked you to forget me. It's only been a few short weeks and now I'm back here, needing you, asking you to let me in after you started to shut me out. The morphine makes me drowsy. "You can love me today," I whisper in your ear, "because I won't remember tomorrow."

I lay on the floor. I'm right beside the bed. I can't get back into it. I had to go to the bathroom and the only way was to crawl, or ask you. But I don't want any more help. I spent the last five days eating only when you brought me food, and sleeping in a haze of drugs. I slid out of bed and hit the floor with a thump, took a second to ground myself, and started to crawl to the toilet. It might have taken half an hour. Or an hour? I don't know. It was painful and slow. I reached down and found a primal place, animalistic. Did I growl on the way? I'm a wolf. The pack crawls with me. Somehow we make it across the bedroom floor. The next obstacle is the bathroom. The toilet seems so far, but the tiles are cool. I rest my head and sway back and forth. I arch my back. Now I'm a cat instead of a dog. I arch and breathe. I breathe into the tight and painful spots, just like they teach in yoga. But the pain is everywhere; my breath gets lost. I can't turn back now, I'm more than halfway there. I want to rest but I can't quit, not until I make it. I wonder what you would think if you came upstairs and saw me slumped on the floor in a puddle of piss, passed out in pain. When I reach the toilet I wonder how I will get up there, how I will climb the porcelain God. Here's another man with power over me. I hold on to the shower stall, grip the wall, and raise myself to almost standing. My knees buckle. I forgot about my pants: I almost sit down with them on. I use one hand to support myself against the shower and the other to pull down my pajama pants. My knees buckle again but it's okay; the toilet is underneath me. What a relief. The journey back takes twice as much time, now that the urgency is gone. The bed looms in front of me, too big to scale. I've done all that I can do alone. I pull the blanket off the bed and use it as a pillow and a cover. I put my head down and close my eyes. The only thing left is to wait for you. To hope you will help me, and trust that you will.

Dear Shawnda,

Okay, 1:30am now. One half hour of distance-healing to you from the universal love energy. Here is what I can feel the messages are to you. You may not feel free tonight, but you will in time. Your energy is muted/softened right now. Animal companions sending themselves through waves of light (I saw this and felt like I wanted to walk close to the floor). Animal companions want to hold you up like with popsicle sticks. This may mean something to you. Heart is heavy like wants to fall through floor. Spine falls forward. Deep heaviness.

Love,

Shirley

I haven't made love to you for weeks. I forgot how delicious it was. You enter my body at only one point and yet manage to spread out everywhere. Your muscles fold around mine until they are bound. Your bones grind into mine until we are fused. The sinews and tissues of you wrap around mine like hungry fingers. Soon, your blood is coursing through my veins. Your heart is beating in tandem with mine, our breathing in sync. I lay with my head lowered, between your knees, overwhelmed with an emotion I cannot name. In a tangled mess I feel a heartbeat, heavy. I think it is mine, but it is not. It is yours. In this moment, feeling your chest rise and fall, I open up and receive you. It's just that easy. It's how I've been made. I think then of your body, and of how you really have to want me for this to happen. You have the control over whether this happens or not. So, technically you had to want her too. If you didn't want her, it wouldn't have happened. It's written all over your body. Like it or not, she's there. You always wanted a threesome.

I tried to stand up on my feet and ended up flat on my back. Is the Universe trying to teach me a lesson ? Trying to show me that I really can't do this. Or is it just a challenge? Should I not have called you? Should I have attempted first to do it on my own? What does it say about me, about us, that I didn't? I never even thought of doing this alone. You were the first person I thought of and the only one I called. Probably the only one who would come. This time I came to you and you were there. Does it matter anymore about the times that you weren't there? Does it? What am I supposed to do now that I've started to feel better and am able to function independently of you? Do I go back home? Do I leave you again? Is that why you don't look at me, don't give me more than the bare minimum I need? Is it because you know this is temporary? But how could you, when I don't even know it yet? Are you preparing yourself just in case, for when, for if, it happens, like the way I used to prepare myself for you to leave me, always aware that the times you were with me couldn't last? That my happiness is always, always temporary?

It's time to go home. I've overstayed my welcome. You got me again. How did I not see this coming? I didn't realize that I was replaceable - thought the opposite, in fact. Thought my leaving you would show you just how much you needed me. Thought your whole world would crash down around you. Thought you'd come begging for another chance. And I thought I would give it to you, when I felt the time was right, when I felt you had suffered enough and that your hurt somehow equaled mine. I didn't expect that you wouldn't need me at all, that instead of being sorry you would actually turn out to be quite mean. All those times you said you loved me - if that love was real, how did it disappear so fast? Without a trace, replaced with disgust? I see it in your eyes.

Maybe we were just cliché. Soulmates. Made for each other. A match made in heaven. Fools in love. Tit for tat. She died of a broken heart. She thought distance would make the heart grow fonder. It didn't.

Yes, it is time to go home. I pack my bags a second time, I take the kids, I leave again. My back is a little stronger now. I'm a little stronger now.

Back to the basement. It's a wonderful world. Really? I hadn't noticed. At least, not in a while. My gratitude journal sits empty, the final entry written weeks ago. I was grateful then for Miss Vickie's Sea Salt and Malt Vinegar chips, for the can of red paint I found in the garage, and for you. But that was then; this is now. Now I wake up alone because you are gone. You're sleeping on the couch, you told me, because you can't sleep without me in our bed. I've eaten all the chips and found they only made me thirsty. I fulfilled one need and created another. And the paint? It's dried-up and unusable. It must have been frozen along with my heart sometime over the past winter when it was neglected and forgotten. Nothing is ever what it seems. Take things for granted, assume they will always be there, and discover how far from the truth that is.

I can force my eyes shut at night but in the daytime I can't get them to open up. I don't sleep, but move in a fog. My brain feels heavy. Fuzzy. Like I can't focus on anything. Another month has passed. A month: that's how long you were with her. I'll never forget that now. I wonder if it was really longer. You were never very good with dates. I bet if I asked her she would know. She would know all the dates. When you met, when you had your first kiss, when you slept with her for the very first time. Oh God. Was it all on the same day? Did all of those things happen on the same night? I forgot to ask you that. Did she want to celebrate, when you made it to a month? Did you take her on dates? Eat in restaurants together and have others think you were a couple? Did you keep your wedding ring on your finger or tuck it in your pocket? Did she know how to make you smile? Did she learn where to touch you to make you call out her name? Did you say it in short, passionate bursts, or in one long syllable, drawing out her name in pleasure while she touched you everywhere? The Enchantress, ever willing to release you from the shackles that kept you bound to me. Was there some other pet name you had for her? Something intimate, shared only between you two? Did you ever call her by my name, if only by mistake? Did you close your eyes sometimes and see me there? Or did she get your full attention? Was I pushed out of your mind? How could you forget me, your family, your life, your future, your wife? Do you see why I can't forgive you? Why this is too much for me to take? I'd rather deal with the sadness of losing you because I chose to leave, than lose you because you choose to leave me. For her. Although I would prefer not to acknowledge the true dark side, intrinsically I know I must embrace this necessary evil gnawing at my pressure points for my own evolution. Be the change I wish to see.

I never realized how angry I was with her. You should have been the one to know better. You never should have given her the opening! But she shouldn't have taken it, shouldn't have crawled up into it. I could almost forgive her, I suppose, if you and I had only been dating. But you said she knew you were married. To me! Which means you told her. You deserve each other then, I think. A married man who ignores his vows, a tramp of a woman who beds a married man. Disgusting, both of you. What, I wonder, does that make me?

Now that we aren't together, I don't have to look into the same eyes that she did. Don't have to be touched by the hands that held her, touched her, opened up her body so you could enter it. Don't have to put my kisses on top of hers. Don't have to wonder if you fucked her and then came home and made love to me, all on the same day.

He stopped calling me recently. I overwhelm him with my neediness. Looking for a part-time lover, he knows that isn't me. I thought it would make me sad, but it doesn't. I'm always chasing love. It eludes me every time. The last time I made love to him - had sex with him, got fucked by him - the last time, I knew that would be it. I saw through the veil that was keeping me blind. I now see the truth. Clear eyes don't see blindly in the morning light. I will never be free. There is always something there to remind me - of you. How can I think of loving him when the love I have for you fills every corner of my heart? It takes up all the space. I could confess my sins in a thousand churches, looking for absolution, but the only thing that matters is how I look in your eyes.

I have never seen myself naked. I think about the men in my life who have stared at a body I am barely familiar with. Men who have handled me roughly and also with tenderness. Men who have loved my body and also complained about it. They have taught me how to treat it, how to ignore it. I think about the men I have shared myself with, allowing them to penetrate deep into my soul and get inside me, physically and mentally. These men have built up my self-esteem and then destroyed it. I think about that for a second: all those men had such authority over what was rightly mine. How dare they presume it was all right by me for them to control each aspect of my being? Or any aspect, for that matter? But they couldn't possibly have known it wasn't okay with me, because I never once spoke up for myself. I never took ownership of my body, never complained when they hurt me, never demanded the truth when they could only speak ugly words about me. I didn't even know my own truth. I let them decide for me what my emotions would be. I should have screamed it from the rooftops: "This body is mine!" Why didn't I love the stretch marks that came as tiny battle scars marking the time my children spent inside of me? Why didn't I embrace my hips or love my breasts? Almost 16 years ago, a man said I had ugly breasts. And I believed him. To this very day I think it's true. But just because somebody says something doesn't mean it's true. How did I forget that? How did I skip over all the years my breasts provided milk to nourish my children and come to focus on a single comment from so many years ago? Who was that guy, anyway? He was someone who should have zero significance, who probably doesn't even think of me anymore - maybe he never did after that day. And here I am, still beating up my body on account of what he said.

I know when it happened, when I stopped caring about my external self. I was 17. It was when my body betrayed me. When it responded in a way I didn't expect.

The front door opens. It slams into the fridge that sits behind it. I am at the sink, washing dishes. I am wearing boxer shorts and a t-shirt. There's a mirror hanging above the sink. I have stopped looking at myself and turn to see who has come in instead of looking up to see the reflection of who entered. I don't know him but I'm not surprised that he just walked in. My roommate allows for such things to happen. It's an apartment drop-in center. He doesn't say much. He has chosen me. I will go with him tonight. Do what he asks. I smile as I protest. There is no choice. I have dishes to wash, pajamas on, no shoes. There isn't a discussion. I have been chosen. He doesn't see me. Doesn't hear me. He stands tall next to me, the top of my head barely past his navel. My heart bleeds. This is going to happen again. "I have a boyfriend," I whisper. It doesn't matter. Makes no difference. He knows it's a lie. He could take me for the night and no one would care. No one would notice. When he realizes I won't walk on my own to his car he swoops and picks me up. Effortless. My hands full of soap suds. I won't walk. I'm in my pajamas. No shoes. I am strapped in by my seat belt. Passenger side. Front seat. It's happening. Again. I have been chosen. We drive and I am lost. I don't speak. Maybe he does. But I don't hear. I try to pay attention, read the street signs. But it's too late. Where is my mother? I'm already lost. I am chosen. I have dishes to wash. Pajamas on.

He parks in front of a small house. I won't walk. I expect the house to be empty, but it's not. An older couple watches TV. Politeness is expected. I do not speak out of turn and answer only when spoken to. They think I am nice. Sweet. I am lost. The woman goes to the kitchen for beer. I know that alcohol numbs. I want to drink quickly, but take in sips slowly. Slowly. I am nice and sweet and lost. The alcohol numbs. Don't they wonder why I am wearing shorts without shoes? A t-shirt and no jacket? It's January. There's snow outside.

My head starts to dip. From the alcohol and my desire to sleep. I am in my pajamas. He leads me downstairs. To the basement. I realize that I have forgotten to say goodbye, goodnight, to the couple in the living room back upstairs. It doesn't matter. They don't wonder where I came from. Where I went. Am I even the first one? Maybe they just don't ask anymore. Maybe they went silent long ago.

The basement is dark. He doesn't turn on the light. Like an animal, he sees through the darkness. Familiar. He whispers in my neck, "Take off your clothes. And wait." I am reeling. "Fuck you," I say. In my head. Not out loud. Anger rises, bubbles for a second before it is pushed away. I am numb again. Take off my clothes. Slide my legs out of the shorts. Underwear. T-shirt. Bra. It is cold in the basement. I am cold and I am lost.

Now I am alone. My eyes adjust. I see a mattress on the floor. A washing machine. A row of beer bottles, empty. I cover my nakedness with my hands. Stand over the bed. It doesn't look scary. It's just a bed. But I'm scared. It's happening again. I'm alone, lost, and cold. In the bed, I sleep. And wake. Sleep. I am cold. Alone. Still. Finally he moves quietly down the stairs. There is nowhere to go. To hide. Nowhere. In one movement he is beside me and inside of me. I have been chosen. I am having unprotected sex with a man that I don't know. I didn't choose this. He moves and moans. I am ripped and raw. He pushes harder. From the side. Flips me over. Pushes and moans. Nowhere to hide. It's happening. He is full of heat. I am cold. He is warm.

Soft. Hard. He pushes, moans. From behind he enters me. For a moment I wonder if he thinks my ass is too wide, too big, too white. He doesn't care. He doesn't know my name. I am chosen. I didn't choose this. I am cold. He is warm. It goes on and on. He pierces my insides. Daggers float up inside of me, past my intestines, stomach, lungs, throat. Explode out of the top of my head. Exploding. The daggers. Filled with heat. His warmth. I am not cold or alone. I explode. Over and over. I am exploding and it's warm. I see light. A bright light. The basement is bright. The bed is wet. I am making the bed wet. I am exploding. I am moaning. My body betrays me. This feels good. It feels nice. I am having unprotected sex with a man I don't know. I am chosen. I didn't choose this. He didn't ask. My body is unfamiliar. Warm. Exploding. Guilty. Lost. My fault this time. It happened again. Guilty. I am confused because I am nice and sweet and wet and betrayed. Betrayed by my very own body. Finally it ends. I sleep and don't wake.

I am late for work. It's dark when I leave for work and now it's light so I know. I am late. Wake up, wake up, wake up. He is sleeping. I am late. Wake up. He doesn't move. I am lost and I am stuck and I am late. I am awake. He holds my neck in his sleep. I can't move. I see a clock. See how late. I am awake and he will sleep and sleep with his arm on my neck until he chooses to wake up. He chooses. I do not. When he wakes I am allowed to put my clothes on. He will take me home.

It is January. There is snow on the ground. I have no shoes. Pajamas on. In the car again. Passenger side. Front seat. He drives and then stops. He is bored with me now. It's over. Time to leave. Get out.

Get out? I repeat. This is the first time I have spoken. Get out? Get out? Get out? I have no shoes. It's January. Get. Out. Out. Out. Out.

I have been dismissed. I open the door. There is snow on the ground. Get. He gives me money for a taxi. Blood money. But it's not enough. The first car drives past. Whatever I am he doesn't want to get involved. Who can blame him? Another passes. And another. Another. Leaving me. In the snow. I am a monster. I am lost and he said he would take me home. I have been dismissed. It's not enough. I am a monster. My feet stick to the snow and I walk on the road. I am not warm and I am not cold. I am numb. I walk on the road and a taxi stops. I close my eyes and lean my head back on the seat. He asks me where I am going and I don't know. He wants an address but I am lost. I belong nowhere. I am numb. I recite a mouthful of numbers and close my eyes until we get to the door. My door. My kitchen. My dishes.

I shower. His pubic hair falls out of me and sits in the tub.

Is this love, is this love, is this love? - Bob Marley plays on the radio.

All these memories wear me down. I can't stop eating. Twenty-four mini boxes of Smarties. Two egg sandwiches. Handful after handful of leftover Halloween candy. A huge plate of chicken with dumplings, yams, and gravy. A bowl of cereal. A package of luncheon meat, then another. Cookie after cookie. And that's just today - so far. I am trying, I realize, to fill the giant gaping hole you have left in my life. I know it's not possible, that I will never be able to eat enough for that to happen. I will always be empty. You were a part of me and now you are gone. There is no way to fix that - or if there is, I don't know what it is. But I just can't stop trying, hoping. My stomach rolls out of my jeans and sits on top. Soon, they won't button. I don't care. I just don't care about anything anymore. What difference does it make?

Your happiness is my compromise. You are free while I am burdened with the life that I have chosen. I remember that there are no sacrifices, only choices as I push my emotions far down, deep into the pit of my stomach, and cover them with food. I wonder what it would be like, to leave this place I started to call home and live only for me. But for the children, I wouldn't have grown these roots that now hold me in place. I'd much rather have wings than roots. Much rather fly than be stuck in one place. Especially here in this place.

I don't want to hurt. I don't want to feel hurt or cause hurt. I love you but I hate me. When will it cease? When will he leave me alone? When will he leave me? Why does the past both haunt and hurt me? My womb aches. I'm still trying after all these years to push him out. I amass dozens of self-help books: I will help them help me. Help me! Who is "me"?

Who am I? What are you, ugly girl in the mirror, who eats to feel full because she is empty? That girl is not me. My eyes sink as the day fades away. Sweetness fills the air. I evaporate into nothing. Goodbye. Goodbye. The wind blows me into sleep. Goodnight instead of goodbye - for now, anyway.

I am sinking. Falling. Into a deep depression. And yet, I wonder why those are the words we choose to describe a feeling that feels more like being stuck. Not sinking or falling. Just glued. In one spot. Trapped and unable to move. While the past catches up with me and the future runs away.

All I want is to crawl into bed, blankets over head in a state of not-quite-depressed but a sort of melancholy born of a longing I can't quite put my finger on. It's the almost-sadness that keeps you attached to your personal story, and keeps you up at night - every night, until even in exhaustion you fail to find rest. It's a state that I've been resisting, even knowing as I do that what you resist persists until this lingering sadness has overstayed its welcome. It's been a good month or more now with no end in sight. It gets to me; it has gotten to me. I am in a funk. I can't get out. I can't get up. I can't wake up and get out of bed. I feel like my head is separate from the rest of me. I hide under the blankets, but keep my eyes open. I'm scared to get up and face another day - another day without you. But I'll do what I have to. What other choice do I have? I have been here before. Many times. Too many times. A depression that lingers, a sadness that never fades. An energy so low I have had to fight, to claw my way back out to some kind of normal.

My hand reaches into a bag of cookies. It's empty. I have eaten the entire bag. Single sitting, one serving. I have eaten them and yet I taste nothing. If it wasn't for the crumbs and stains I might be able to convince myself the bag was empty when I sat down. The only thing that is empty is me. And no amount of cookies can make me whole. But maybe there is safety in that extra layer of fat. I feel it forming. No one can reach me now. Each pound gained and lost and gained again until I spew the truth.

Sometimes I can't get up in the morning. My legs, lead-heavy, sink into the mattress. They just won't move. Depression. That's not me. Depression means sad, but I am not sad. I am frozen. Stuck and melting all at the same time. Depressed. Deep rest.

I could sleep forever and not even know that the day had passed. It's so dark, down here in the basement. Without the moon I am lost. There's no window in the kitchen, or the bathroom. In the bedroom there is a tiny one, but it's under the deck so it barely counts. The living room has a door: my only source of light. I picture myself crawling up to the door sometimes, pressing my face against the glass to feel the warmth of the sun, my arms reaching out for it like the plants always did at home. Stretching their little bodies, twisting up to reach the light. Sometimes I'd try to trick them, would turn their pots around. But they would only laugh at me, turn their arms around, and reach in the other direction. They knew what they needed to survive. All the things I thought I needed I no longer have - but I'm still here, still alive. I think I need darkness right now. Maybe I'm just a tiny seed, burrowed deep in the soil, waiting for just the right moment. Maybe I will know just the right time to emerge from my tight shell, and will push forward without any external direction. I'll make my way out. Find the sun, reach for the sky - someday. But first, darkness. Stillness. Quiet reflection. Inner growth before outer growth.

A new moon. Today is darkness. The moon is hiding. It's just as well. She can only witness. Not testify.

I used to play a little game with you. When you were busy, with your attention somewhere else, I would try and see if I could get you to look at me. I would concentrate really hard. Stare at you. Look at me. Look at me. I'd only ever say it in my mind. Then I'd pause and wait. See if you would look. When you didn't, I would try harder. I'd fix my gaze somewhere on your face. I'd will the words right into you. Forcefully, but silently commanding your attention. Time would pass and you wouldn't flinch. Wouldn't look to see me, wouldn't feel the heat of my stare. Never, not once, could I make you look at me. I realize - real eyes, real lies - that there were very few times when you would look at me at all. I was always trying to generate some connection with you, whether physical or emotional. Aside from those times when I'd try to make you look at me for fun, there were other times when I'd look at you and wait for some reaction. But it never came. Like when I'd look at you with sadness, tears rolling out of my eyes. I used to want you to see the hurt that you put there, to see just what you did. And when I was angry I'd shoot poison daggers with my eyes. Emanate hatred, not from my lips but from between my narrowed lashes. But it all seemed in vain, for even then you wouldn't look. Expressively my eyes would change color for you. I wore my heart on my sleeve, my emotions easily read. But just in case you had some trouble, one look in my eyes and it would all be clear. Green when I was sad. Blue when I was happy. Grey when I was angry. How did you miss that? It was just like me to match my emotions with my eyes, like matching my handbag with my shoes. You never saw it, though; you never saw me.

It always takes me a second to remember that everything good is past-tense now. Although I can't say I'm sorry about it, right now I'm just sorry for me. Because I didn't deserve this, even if you did.

In a dream I drive your work van. Someone breaks the side mirror that you were watching me from. Your image of me is shattered. Some man will charge $100 to fix it. But you think it's worth only $60. What about me? What am I worth to you?

I sit in the front seat of a car in this new dream. How can I dream so often when it seems I never sleep? You whisper, "I am getting there." Where, I wonder? There is nowhere to go. You understand. I twist my (intact) review mirror so I can see you sitting in the back. You ask me if I drink or do drugs. I look you square in the eye and boldly say no. As I move from dream to dream I hear a voice say something. I struggle to hear it, to remember. "This is life," it says. "What you think is life is just moving from dream to dream." I am awake and inside my dream. I wake up and it's still a dream.

Later, I watch a movie. The Butterfly Effect is profound. So many choices, so many possibilities. Can you ever get it right? What happens when you don't? It all continues, goes on. For the others there is more of the same. The ripples are endless. I wonder how "my" choices affect the others. I think of what you say about not choosing and the choices that get made for you. For a moment, I am sad. But mostly I'm sad for them.

He avoids me like the plague. I understand. I tried and tried until it became ridiculous. I'll never play the fool again. I know what he wants from me. And I know what I want isn't him. It makes me sad. Just a twinge - more sad for what I hoped he would be, less sad for what was lost. I think I was behaving like a silly teenage girl. For so many years it was you, only you. When someone else came along and made me feel for the first time in a long time that I was worth something, I got a little giddy. It went straight to my head. I think about Kirk. He told me I was pretty. He was the third man that I slept with, but the first one that I chose. Did it start way back then? This feeling of worth all tied up in a man? In his opinion. If someone tells me I'm beautiful, does it mean I am beautiful? If you make love to me, will it make you love me? Help me to love me?

The seasons change. I change. I've flip-flopped back and forth long enough. It's time for resolution. The leaves on the trees fall and die. Parts of me fall and die too. I hope the parts that are falling are just the ones I don't need any more. I hope all the parts of me don't disappear with the end of summer. Soon it will be winter: a time of reflection, hibernation. A period of time frozen and standing still, moments encapsulated in tiny icy crystals, ready to be examined. Nothing grows in this period. Nothing flowers or blooms. There is only stillness and ice. There is very little sunlight to brighten the days, there are long, lonely nights. There is the cold, and the bitterness and emptiness of the world reflected back in shades of gray. Monochromatic. How fitting that my new life begins in this time, the time between fall and winter, between death and stagnation. First I must shed the layers and then pause to reflect. I have hope that this time is my time just to rest. To take all of my energy and keep it inside until I find the strength to grow again. It's only change. I am safe. The winter season can be long, but it ends every year. It always does. And with the spring, a new beginning comes - my new beginning, a few short months away, I hope. For now I will breathe into the stillness of the icy cold. I will have faith that the days won't always be this chilly, this alone. For just like the bears, I too will come out of hibernation. I will awaken from a deep sleep and see that there is some divine plan. Some sense in nonsense.

Christmas is coming. It's just around the corner. It was always my favorite holiday. The holiday of abundance, the holiday of family. I wouldn't open my gifts until you had opened all of yours. I liked to watch and see what expressions of joy I could create with a simple package. Loved to listen to the kids squeal in delight and catch a glimpse of what it must have been like - or rather what it should have been like - to be a child myself. That in itself was always the best gift to me. My presents, I knew, would always be exactly what I asked you for anyway. I would give you a wish list and you'd use it as a shopping list. Even though I told you it wasn't about the gifts, you always spent too much. Was that how you showed me love? By buying things you knew I'd like? Maybe you wanted me to have the things on my list, but maybe you had to stick with the list because you didn't know me well enough to pick anything else.

I'm not very good at reading my own cards. I tried sleeping with a deck of tarot cards under my pillow for a week. I wanted to suffuse each card with my deepest thoughts. I hoped that what the future holds for me might be revealed, might be more clear. I wanted to give myself valuable life advice since so far, all I seemed capable of was making a mess of everything. I wanted to do a full spread, not just select one card, like what I do with you. But I needed my instruction book to remember the layout. Tarot for Beginners. An easy guide. Sure, this book might help me decipher the cards, but what to do with the advice is not for beginners, nor is it easy. But today I just need a guide, so I pick up my book and it falls open. Funny how the answers just appear in front of you. Ask and ye shall receive. All you have to do is be open to it - open a book. I get King of Swords: a man of power and authority. A man who might appear to be an ally, or disguise himself as your lover. A man who puts his own interests first. Justice in his view is whatever benefits himself. His is not a balanced scale; it is tipped how he sees fit. Isn't that just like you? Putting your own interests first and condemning me when I try to find balance?

Everyone who's been in my shoes, who's loved and lost and loved again, will say that time heals all wounds. Instead of disappearing, the wounds are covered in scar tissue - thick enough to hide the pain. But I keep waking up, waiting for it to be just like it was, hoping it's all a dream and that you are right here, next to me. You never are, of course, because like always I am here and you are there. This time though, there is a physical distance between us too, not just emotional space. I'm giving it time. But everything is still all about you. Nothing feels right anymore. I can't move on when I am still looking back to when I had you. "Come back," I whisper in the dark. "Come back." But you weren't the one who left; it was me. And if I ask myself to do the same thing, to "come back?" the answer is no, I can't go back. I can only move forward.

I didn't miss you much today. Hardly thought of you at all. Maybe I don't need you as much as I thought, as much as I feared. Maybe I am okay just all on my own. Maybe I am fine, thank you very much. I didn't even cry today. Not one single tear. Happiness is still a stretch, but no longer a leap. Am I only fooling myself? Will I wake up tomorrow and find that my heart aches just like it did yesterday? It seems already like so long ago, when I loved you and you loved me back. When my whole life was you. I do still wonder what you do now without me, when you get home at night from work and find I'm no longer there. But now it's almost like a curious question, not a burning desire accompanied with a need to know. My back aches, though. Hurts like a son of a bitch.

Pinching and stabbing. Throbbing. Maybe I just need to get you off my back. Maybe, like my good friend Louise says in her Heal Your Life workbooks, my back aches because I have unresolved issues in my relationship. Perhaps, Louise, perhaps. Or maybe I really am over you, over this, and it's just my cheap mattress causing the discomfort. It could even be growing pains. I guess only time will tell.

I wonder if I should start telling people that I left you. You have told your friends and most of your family by now, I'm sure. I wonder how you told them, what you said. Do they think it's my fault, do they feel sorry for you? I have told only one person and I didn't like the way the words sounded as they rolled off my tongue, so I never spoke them aloud again. Not to anyone. I can't bear to think of this as permanent. Maybe I just need practice. So the next time I'm at the grocery store I tell the cashier. "Cash or debit?" she asks me. "I left my husband," I reply. I wait for the world to come crashing down around me. It doesn't. The cashier blinks. "Cash or debit?" she asks again. Her line is getting long, she hasn't had her lunch break yet, one of her kids is sick, and her sitter has to leave early. I don't know any of this because of course she doesn't air out her dirty laundry in the grocery line like I just did. But I sense her frustration and since the world didn't end like I thought it might when I spoke, I can only answer her question and not ask any of my own. What I really would have liked to ask her was if she thought I'd made a mistake. If I should go back. If it will get easier. If you ever really get used to sleeping alone when for over a decade you slept all tangled up in someone's arms. I don't know why, but I think she has the answers. I can see it in her face. "Debit," I whisper softly, thinking that D word is much easier to say than another one I know. Divorce.

I went to a naked photo shoot, had pictures done of my Self. I wanted to see for sure if I was beautiful. And now I know I am. It seemed kind of shady at first; his studio was in a basement. My memories echoed and for a moment I am numb. But he had a set and proper lighting. Once I was there it was kind of too late anyway. How do you tell someone, "I'm not sure if I trust you"? Sudden, I know. Our rapport was always so good before. But you are a stranger. This is a basement. I haven't had any alcohol. He didn't have much to say. Just told me where to sit. Where to stand. What to put on. What to take off. This time there are no pajamas. My underwear stays on until I'm ready. There are even strappy shoes in the wardrobe, my feet not bare this time. And there are necklaces around my neck instead of hands. It was very technical. Why was I so emotional? He didn't look at me, though. Not in a strange or creepy way. It was all lighting and shadows. No dirty mattress. No empty beer bottles. I don't know how to stand without covering my body. There are so many flaws, but I only have two hands. I didn't start out nude, of course; I worked my way there slowly. Strange how you still feel naked in front of the camera, even when you have clothes on. It's surreal, the experience of seeing myself through the lens. It was like being at my dentist, where I'd watch my reflection in his glasses, getting to see how I looked through someone else's eyes. This was different, though, because what the photographer saw got recorded. Captured. He caught me naked. With clothes on. Seeing with his eyes. He tried a few times to show me the images on the back of his digital camera. I didn't look at them. Couldn't. Could not bear to look at myself that exposed, that vulnerable. I'd tell him they were nice. What else could I say? Except he took offense to this. "Nice."

What did that say of his work? Is there a compliment in there? He didn't think so. "But go on, take a second look." And when I did, when I really did look, they were breathtaking. She was beautiful. I...was beautiful. He said it too, in awe. "This is so beautiful." "What," I asked, "the photos or me?" "The photos of you," he answered. "The photos are you."

There's a purple flower in the backyard. It bloomed just the other day. Came out of nowhere. All summer long the clematis looked dead. I'd be in the kitchen, washing your dishes and thinking to myself "I really should go dig that up." But I was always too busy. Taking care of you didn't leave time for much else. You can imagine how surprised I was to see it bloom after all the other flowers had died, after the first flakes of snow were already on the ground. One brilliant purple bloom. On the dead plant. There's not even one leaf alive. It looks so pretty out there, the edges folding in slightly because of the cold. A backdrop of passion on the virgin snow. It's as big as my hand. A dazzling display of color.

I am dreaming. The moon rays extend behind me, in front of me, through me. I take my hands and dip into the light. Surprised, I find my hands are wet. Soaked with the milk my mother never shared with me. I dip down and scoop up handfuls to wash my face. Cleansing. I dip again. First my hands, and then my whole body follows. I swim in the milk bath until I reach the end of the pool. I climb onto a tiled ledge. Looking first left and then right I contemplate which way to go next. I hesitate because there are doors on either side and yet there is no indication of what I might find once I pass through them. I am pleased to discover a third choice. A doorway at my feet opens up to reveal a lush, green rainforest. I may enter, but only if I fall. There is another pool in front of me and I know I want to swim but can't remember if I do. It's time to come back.

I meditate. I am moving up through the chakras. Each one is a lotus flower, opening and closing with my breath. The Muladara chakra, my root chakra: the very first one, my base, my foundation. It glows red. The second is orange. And so on, up the sequence of the main seven. It's difficult to focus on the colors. I only see white. A glowing white light, just to the left of me. Outside of me. My lotus flowers breathe. The white light intensifies. My base chakra still glows red.

The white light, brilliant and intense but not intrusive, moves closer to me. My eyes are closed. I feel the light hesitate and hover just outside the left side of my head. It enters my third eye. Now the white light is inside of me. It feels warm. I play with the color wheel inside of me, changing my focus from the red roots right up to the crown, where it's blue. The white light dances through the colors. It's playing with me, I realize. I smile because I am not alone. Someone or something has come to play with me, to make their presence known. Maybe it's my angel. A ball of energy, dancing in and around my chakras. The red becomes less intense, almost orange. The purple fades to a light blue. Adding white light changes everything, gives a whole new perspective. It feels light, airy. I haven't felt this close to happy in quite some time. I almost remember what it's like to feel good. Almost.

The light of the moon washes over me, flooding the room. She is so very full. She is widening her circle of wisdom, stretching higher. Like her, I rise and fall. Wax and wane. I watch her chase the sun each day. The yang to her yin, her one true love, always just out of reach. When she gets there, it's already too late.

He already left. Couldn't he just wait? One day, could he wait, for only a few hours, until she catches up with him? But he thinks only of himself. He doesn't even notice her. My body moves in cycles like her. It's time to pay attention. Wild horses couldn't drag the sun down and make him wait, and wild horses couldn't hold you either. We look at each other, night after night. Me, gazing up. She, peering down. Perhaps we could find comfort in each other. But we don't. Each of us is consumed with a love unrequited.

Goodbye, goodbye, innocence, value, respect, trust. Goodbye. I am reading a book called Cunt. I think about my own. This part of me to which I have no connection. Folds of skin hidden under a bushel of coarse, dark hair. A secret soft place. A starting point. A journey towards the center of me. Covered with my soulskin. Having sex is different for a woman, my mother would sometimes say. He becomes a part of you. None of the men I had slept with were part of me. That down-there place wasn't sacred, loved, or cherished. When I was sixteen my soulskin was ripped away. Stolen. None of the men, except you, became part of me. You were the only one I truly let in. When will my vagina be more than just a hole? I almost wrote whole. When will my vagina be whole?

I think back to the birth of my children. The lingering disconnect from the feminine me. How I shit all over the birth table because I didn't know which muscles to relax. How the ring of fire was the first sensation I had down there that I couldn't disappear or dream myself away from. How even then, even then, I couldn't get past function and into form. I could birth myself a baby, but not create an architecturally sound vagina. Still a hole. Not quite whole. Even the word: vagina. A sheath to enclose a stem. My oldest daughter called it a pokey. Poke. He. To the younger girls it was a Betty. Closed tight like purse strings on the old lady's bag. But to me, it was a vagina. A sheath to enclose a stem, a shaft. Made from a split piece of wood. It was certainly not mine, it was just a gaping hole. When will I be whole?

The past is over. How can it still haunt me so, if this is true? The inner creates the outer. My inner world is in a disastrous state. What is the sound of my soul? I can't even hear it anymore. All I hear is my heart beating in fear. I'm afraid to be alone. So desperately alone. Alone. Loner. Lonely. What will I do to fill the hours if I don't spend my time thinking of you, taking care of you, wondering what is the next thing and the next thing and the next thing I have to do to make sure you stay happy? What is the next line in my story? Broken in two, half of me stays with you. It refuses to move ahead, can only see the loss. Feel it. The other half knows this much is true: that she must go on, she must. What else can she do? The wishbone. I am - again.

Stagnant water has no life. Water. I am made of water. Water is meant to flow. Go with the flow. Roll with the punches. Accept change. Don't force or fight. Waves of warmth wash over me. I am not alone. I have myself. Always have me. Remember, in acceptance you find forgiveness. And that doesn't mean I have to be a victim. The truth is, this is all in the past now, and I am only alive within my own mind. If I am a victim now, it is only of my thoughts and judgments. It might also just mean that you were too wrapped up in your own world, the one I was barely a part of, to notice the hurt you inflicted. There's always another side to the story. Even if I can only see mine right now. I am starting to be present. I am letting go of the illusion.

I will try an experiment. I will eat nothing unless I am able to do so mindfully. How can I, though, when my mind is a place I don't want to be? Right now, I'm comfortably numb. The food keeps me numb. My emotions are pushed deep down to fill the places my insecurities used to be. They don't have to hide anymore. They dance around me now that they have been confirmed. Justified.

I realize I do exist without him. My marriage will never be the same, will never be what it was. But that's a good thing. Before this, I was fixed and frozen. This has shifted me towards a new future. Whether we were together or alone, things couldn't have stayed the same. I am embracing change. I realize that trust doesn't have to be something you give away. Trust yourself: that's all you need. I have a circle of friends around me. How am I alone? Alone. Al one. All one. See the bigger picture. I can be alone with myself and it's not as terrible as I feared. Look on the bright side: not sleeping at night helps me get a lot of stuff done around the house. Sleep is overrated anyway.

Even if I can't forgive just yet, I am on a journey towards it. I am starting to understand that forgiveness is not for you, it's something I need to do for me. Forgiving you doesn't have to mean I condone the event, just that I accept that it happened, that I see it for the experience that it was. It exists on its own, outside of me, has two sides, both yours and mine. I am awakening, and once your eyes are open, you can't close them again.

The winter is long. It's a solstice of relief. I have completed my teacher training; I am certified to teach yoga. Finally, I finish one thing that I started. I teach my first class. We meditate with chocolate, bringing our feet into easy cross-legged pose, closing our eyes. We straighten our spines and imagine opening the crowns of our heads as we lengthen, radiating up to the sky. We root our sit bones. We take a piece of chocolate, hold it, let it linger in our hands for a minute or so. Feel the weight. Think of how the life of our whole planet and sun are contained in the chocolate. Now we gently place it on our tongues, keeping our jaws relaxed. The mouth is a sacred point of nutrition and the place where we express our Selves. It offers communion and is a source of great pleasure. Once it's inside, we let the chocolate melt and fill us with sweetness. We taste the value and meaning in our lives in that melting piece of chocolate. We meditate on the chocolate plant, on the work of the farmer, on the many thousands of children who die each day for lack of food. We feel it melting, and as we swallow, we feel it become part of us. We ask our Selves this: Am I enjoying all aspects of my life, even the difficult moments, in similar fashion? Pause here. Am I fully aware? Look for the good. Accept the bad. It will balance. It has to.

I am bliss.

I am bliss.

Bliss absolute.

Bliss I am.

I think of my own affair, of the few times I shared my body with him. I think of how empty it felt, how it lacked intimacy, how hard I tried to make him you. How each and every time he touched me I'd flinch - because he wasn't you. I suppose that's not quite true; there were times when I didn't flinch, but melted instead at the heat of his touch. Those were the times when I thought we shared intimacy and felt full with what he gave me. There were times when I'd share my body with him and the reasons always seemed clear: I wanted to hurt you, get back at you, give you the gift of understanding. Here, have some hurt. Feel it like me. "Oh, so that's what it feels like. Now I get it. Now I won't do it to you again. Ever." Would you ever say that to me?

Hindsight is twenty-twenty. I thought I could give you your lessons, forgetting of course that you must learn them yourself. I tried to create intimacy and left feeling so empty, ever so empty. It almost hurt me more than you. Do I want to control or respond to my emotions? Am I addicted to this state? No one has the power to do that, to hurt me - or no one should, but I gave that power to you. I acquiesced it.

Who will give me my lessons? It's time to see that my perception of the world alters my experience of it. Let's start with forgiveness; that seems like a good place to begin. I think of my tiny son, and of the lessons he teaches me on a daily basis. He brought the theme of forgiveness into my life. With him, I passed a series of tests that seemed enormous at the time but are really quite tiny in comparison to the final exam: the forgiveness I have to give you. Forgiveness that begins with the birth of our son. He is here to bring us together, somehow. The cut umbilical cord severed my physical connection to him three months ago, but an invisible attachment remains, grows, and is strengthened. My body pours an abundance of milk, at his demand, filling him to overflowing until content. We rest. Moving in silent ebbs and flows, a short time later we join again as mother and son. He is me. I am him.

He is the physical manifestation of my own toxicity. I am leaking poison. Draining it straight into him. He is me. I am him. An itchy spot spreads on his skin. First pink, then red. Angry. Hot. He scratches, digging at his skin, unable to get relief. His cheeks look slapped. His tiny mouth is pursed in a silent "oh." Without complaint, he rubs his legs back and forth against each other, against the sheets, searching for an end to this persistent itchiness. Eczema. It covers him. It bleeds up to his eyes. Angry whorls fester and split. His skin is raw, cracked, oozing. First blood and then pus. I scale back the bath products and change the laundry soap. I rub soothing ointments, slather his skin with oils, and whisper softly to him.

His skin gets worse. I realize that my milk, his only source of nourishment, is a probable cause. I eliminate dairy, nuts, corn, soy, wheat, chocolate, citrus, tomatoes, sulphites, meat, sesame, additives, and preservatives, until finally in desperation I have reduced my diet to vegetable patties and water. And yet still, his tiny body is covered in sores.

I start getting funny looks at the grocery store. After a few months people want to know why I haven't fixed it yet. The family doctor pushes cortisones, refers me to a dermatologist who blends a stronger batch. I refuse to use the harsh prescriptions on his delicate skin. "But the cause," I whisper, "the cause." But after several months of this no one is really listening to me anymore.

I bring him to see a Naturopath, am surprised when she doesn't ask to see his skin. I wonder what she will suggest to remedy his pain.

At night I don't sleep anymore, I confess to her. I rub his legs to quell the restlessness so he can get a break. These past few months have changed me too. I am a hollow pod of what I used to be. My restricted diet forced my own body into detox and boils have begun to fester on my skin too.

I am not yet ready, so she suggests it's my deodorant. Stop using hair dye. Get rid of your microwave. Exercise. Drink chrysanthemum tea. Eat more protein. She gently balances his energy and incredibly, he sleeps.

A few weeks later there are still no outward changes to his skin. Is it even possible - could it be worse? We see her again. I want to show her the cracks that stretch endlessly across his chest. But it's me that she looks at. It's me that she talks to. "Forgiveness," she says. A mouthful in one word. A word that makes me itchy. My son's energy is still so fused with mine that she cannot tell which one of us needs to be worked on. I forgot for a moment that he is an old soul and pause for a second to think of him entering my body.

"She doesn't know I am coming, but here I am. I am light. I am love. I enter her body and decide to stay this time. I have chosen her. I love her smile enough to make it mine too. I will like the same flowers she does and I will love music too. In a few months, I will quietly enter her world. I will move gently through her broken body to be her son."

Lost in silence, the truth begs to be told. A new baby grew in a body infected with past hurts. I am numb and can't yet feel the life growing inside of me, oblivious to my pain, absorbing it. I am detached. Vibrationally stuck. And now, a surprise pregnancy. There is no joy. Is my decision the best one? I feel pain. My abdomen stretches. The infection spreads, the IUD floats, and the baby - somehow, the baby swims.

I blink and find myself still in her office. "Forgiveness," she says again. Issues of the skin can almost always be attributed back to the need for forgiveness. Mentally I calculate the list - the long list - of everyone I am angry at. Mad enough it makes my blood boil. Boils. Angry enough that it feels hot and red, almost oozing out of me. I start to see the connection. I am ready.

I need forgiveness. Not from someone else as I originally thought, but from within. I need to forgive me. And so I try.

Each day for a week, I write one letter. At least, that's my plan. I didn't realize how painful and difficult those letters would be, how each one would tear me down until I rested in some deep, dark place inside of me that has never seen the light of day. Somewhere down in the pit of my existence. A very primal place, a place where parts of me still cry for my mother — even though she, too, is on the list. This is a place where wounds never heal, where they are raw and bleeding. It is where unspeakable acts are remembered, where cheating husbands are a walk in the park. The memories down there are far worse than that, and in fact down there they aren't even memories. There is just a string of bad days that repeats over and over. There's a little girl who lives there. A teenager, who is sixteen forever. And a grown woman who walks on a thin layer of ice. Below it, near the surface but covered with scabs, is anger.

It's an emotion none of them - the child, the girl, the woman - ever feel, for they are too lost in sadness and pain. It's a place where flowers don't bloom, where it's always cold. Where love is never felt or shown. It's an ugly, awful place. It's where the little girl, the teenager, and the woman spend their days picking scabs back open to reveal the bloody insides. I don't want to be there, but once you are there, the only way out is through it. Right through the shit. I will go through it, I will write the letters. With whom shall I start? I come up with a list of names.

Writing down the names is enough for one day. I am trying, really I am. In the long run, I will be healthier, will be better able to take care of myself. And this will make me a better, stronger, healthier friend, mother, and wife. I'm doing good for my family, looking at the world with compassion. I didn't realize how difficult it could be to have compassion - not only for those we love and care about, even strangers (who are easy to love) but even for those who have caused us great pain and suffering. Not an easy task at all.

Even the dedication is difficult. Writing down the list of names of every person in my life who has scarred me, who has hurt me so unbelievably that I still carry the wounds deep in my core, whose words have become part of the essence of me, whose actions have stripped me raw and left me reeling. They've left me barely able to breathe - just like right now; I can hardly breathe as I make this list. A list of names: I dedicate this practice to them. May they find peace and happiness.

Dear T,

How much I have hated you over the years. Given so much power to you. Cried for the innocence you took from me. That was my gift. You had no right to rip it away from me. I was whole and you left me broken. It's been fifteen years. Fifteen years of constant thought. Have you ever, even once, thought of me? I doubt it. So why am I holding on to what will never change, what can never be undone? Where I begin and end and where you begin and end is just a blur. The top of your thumb has a top. And that top has a top too, doesn't it? So where does it end? Where does it actually begin? I can't be angry anymore. Can't hold this furious rage in my soul for even one more day. I release it. I am letting go. I have been worried that a small explosion might occur — or even a big one. But no, the anger just fizzles and dies. It never disappears. Think of how much good I can do with the negative energy once it's been redirected. I paused in writing this to nurse my son. My tiny, perfect, spiritual teacher. I was doing this for him, but this should be for me. I feel the knot loosen just a tad. I forgive you. I can't change your energy; I don't know what karmic events led you to make the choices you have. But it's time for me to move on. I don't want to be angry anymore. So I'm letting go. My anger, instead of a ferocious beast, an angry wild animal, is just a simple bird. A songbird with a story to tell. A bird who will fly away and carry all the hurt with it. Bye bye - and whoosh, it disappears. Now I too am like a bird. Free. My forgiveness is yours. I give it to you. Not easily. But honestly. And just in time. Goodbye.

My son. His face clears first. Then, his torso and back. I start eating wheat again and hold my breath. His arms clear. As I nourish my spirit his hair starts to grow back. His face gets chubby. His skin a wonderful shade of brown. Soft and smooth. We are a work in progress, him and me. There are setbacks along the way. Change is never easy. But the rawness has healed. He is me. I am him.

Dear mom,

I can't even capitalize mom. To me, you aren't important. I'm not even sure I want to give you the same title as me. I am Mom, Mother, Mommy. You are none of those to me. Oh dear. Should I start again? This is supposed to be a letter of forgiveness to you. Already there is bitterness erupting. It's a lot to swallow. There's so much to forgive. At least, that's what I still think.

Because you never did it, I will nurture myself. I will mother the small child who resides inside of me by letting her play with all of my children. I'll be the child she never got to be. Each time she resists when it's time for bed, knowing bedtime could be a scary time, I will tuck her gently into bed under a blanket of forgiveness. Then she will sleep safely while I watch. I will love her in place of you. Love her in spite of you. Teach her only how to forgive you. Because now, I know how to do it myself.

And that's when I realize, after a string of false starts and torn-up letters, that I do know how to do it myself. This is about me, not you. Forgiveness is not a grandiose gesture written on a piece of paper. It's a living, breathing document of choice. Forgiveness is not something you give to someone else - it's a gift you give yourself. It's not an act or an action. It's an attitude. It's not a backed-down surrender to justify the choices of another. I don't have to understand or explain your actions, I just have to release myself from the power they hold. And with that, the letters cease. The healing truly begins. All can be forgiven.

And now it's your turn. I have written many letters to you over the past year and a half, but none of them ever made it into your hands. I went to your house the other morning. "Your house" - I can call it that now and it feels okay. I went like I always do, but this time it was different. I've been away long enough now that it doesn't feel like my space anymore. It's oppressively you. Your dishes in the sink. Your clothes on the floor. I left months ago and you still haven't bothered to put a sheet on the bed. The mattress is bare. The pillow is too. I think of my own bed. It's tiny but perfect, with a white feather duvet and dozens of pillows. I sleep there and I'm snug. Safe. I look at your sweater, still on the floor, and I realize I don't have any desire to pick it up and put it on. I find comfort and security in other places now. I don't need them from you, not anymore. I used to want something tangible. Something to hold. I realize now that I don't have to hoard anything. I will always be given exactly what I need in the time and place I need it. Happiness is not an external condition. I used to spend hours thinking of the things that I could do to make you happy. I knew what you wanted before you did, half the time. I could anticipate just what you needed, at any given moment, to bring you pleasure. For years, what you needed was me. The mistake, of course, was giving you so much of me I almost didn't have anything left in the end. I realize that what I was doing was giving to you what I needed for myself. I wanted someone to love me unconditionally - so I gave that to you. I wanted someone to be there for me, in sickness and in health, for better or for worse - so I gave those things to you. They are the things I promised you, and I would have given them anyway, married or not. Because they were the things I wanted, for me. You tricked me by pledging the same things. Perhaps you had the best intentions at the time - I really believe you did. But you can keep your promises, and your lies. I don't need them anymore. I guess trying to write this letter was my way of saying goodbye to the past, and up until today I haven't been quite ready to do that. But then, this never really was about you at all, was it?

So now it's my turn. I forced my mistakes on someone else. Followed when I should have led. Dreamt but never lived. Risked but never tried. Took the easy route. Slept instead of cleaning. Ate food I didn't want. Gave up hope. Stopped believing. I hated that girl, and she was me. I ignored her and pushed food down in her face to quiet the rages. I basked in the forgetful state of nothing. I want nothing, I steal everything, I hurt everyone, and I don't care. I tried to protect you from all my emotions, thinking you wouldn't want the mess of them, the outbursts of hidden pain. I thought perhaps you couldn't handle the truth of me and so I kept it to myself. In the end, I had no sense of who I was until it all spilled out in front of you that day, until I read the clues I left with him. The wildness, the rawness; an eventual erasure of it all. I let you see me as wife material, not the broken mess I was. I gave you my fidelity when my desire was to fuck all the men in the world before they fucked me first. I preached self-love and I hated myself. But all this stops when I say it does. I choose. You do not. And I choose now.

Love heals all hurts. Knowing this, I pause and reflect. I'm lucid. Alive in my dream-state, I dream of my daughter. In the dream she has a secret. I know her. She is all of us. I know her secrets and yet even as I beg her to share she is silent. I reach in towards her chest and pull out straw. Like most of us, she wants to unburden herself from the fear and pain but finds comfort in its presence. She is young and hasn't learned yet how to run. Not yet a flight risk, she holds the pain inside and now I have it in my hand. It is alive - more alive, even, than she is - and her pain dances like fire. It demands attention, sucks the life force until she is drained. She is a reflection of me and of you, and I wait for her lessons to be revealed. The dream continues. I crouch beside her. "You have to share your secrets, let them out," I tell her. The straw in my hands becomes warm. "You have to share," I say, "so that we can learn to take the fear and give it love." Gently, with such tenderness, I look towards this girl, this tiny reminder of what I once was - what we all once were - before the perception of sadness took the wonder from the world. I hold in my hands all of her fear. "Take your fear and give it love." What a simple reminder! For nowhere can the two exist. Engulfed in love, the fear fades. This is a powerful reminder that you can heal yourself. We can all heal our Selves.

We are all Liliths, waiting on the dark side of the moon, hiding from the Man in the Moon though craving his yang to balance our yin. I reflect on the night I sat with the woman at the beach, and of the letter I gingerly placed on the seat of her car - while up on the moon, Lilith crawled over to the Man's face, danced in the craters of his eyes, traced the outline of his nose, dared to kiss his lips. No longer chasing the sun, but realizing that the man next to her, the man in the moon, was so much a part of her that he'd always be there. Before, I was convinced that the letter was hers. But now I am sure it is for me too. Although I had written it I didn't see that it was mine. My very own letter of forgiveness. Just in time.

I am in your city. I sit at the lighthouse and write letters for strangers. I keep our love alive by sharing it with others. I try to honour the teachings you freely gave. I think of you not with sadness or loss, but with love and gratitude. Thank you.

Sometimes you jump. And sometimes, you just need a push. You might not remember what freedom feels like. Lost in the dream, many things are overlooked. But don't worry, the clarity will come. The path to getting there is right in front of you. The clues are found in the synchronistic details, the everyday events of life we often disregard.

I bow to you. Again and again. Your teachers are everywhere too. Do you have gratitude for the lessons they bring? Do you remain grateful when the lessons are perceived as painful, hurtful, more than you can take even? Fear not, for you will never be given more than you can handle. I promise you that. Want to know how I can say that with absolute certainty? Because none of this is real. It's all an illusion. The past that haunts you exists only in your mind, as does the future you plan for and fear so much. The only moment is now. All you are is here.

So the sadness, expressed in this temporal state, and the tears, however convincing, are illusions. The idea that the pain of our existence brings aloneness and isolation - just tricks of the mind! Perhaps you will consider that in the depths of such sorrow, you are closer than ever to home. Hidden in such pain is the path to Heaven, to freedom. All else exists in mind. Only in mind. And you were never alone. Believe me, for I am here.

I see you standing on the edge. Watch you move closer until your toes hang over. I wait to see if this time you will jump, take the leap of faith and just dive right in. But then I see the fear. It's still in your eyes. It holds you back every time. You get so close: almost, almost. I raise my hand in a gesture of encouragement, thinking perhaps if I offer you something tangible to hold then you will not be afraid, that you will be brave just for the moment it will take for you to jump, and that when you do you will discover you have wings.

But when I raise my hand, an offering meant for you, it bumps into glass. It's the mirror image in front of me. I had forgotten: you are but a reflection of me.

And suddenly the teachings I have thoughtfully considered take on new meaning. It's a game of solitaire. There is no other. If you fail, I fail. I fall, you fall. We're all in this together. Our journey is so interconnected that I dream of you at night, when my subconscious carries me home and I dream hallucinations of reality.

That's why I'm cheering for you. That's why I'll hold your hand if you choose to wait for a little bit more. That's why I'll be here to celebrate when you finally find your way back home. I'm here, sending love, shining the light, loving you most when you want it the least. Because I don't make it unless you do. It's an invisible buddy system. No toy gets left behind. No soul walks alone.

There is no right or wrong, no judging your decision: that's the beauty of free will and the wonder of the game. But before you leave the room, can I ask you to do one thing? Please turn on the light, to guide the others who will follow, trying to find the way home just as you have searched. For where would you be now if no one had done that for you?

Gratitudes

I am overflowing with gratitude for each and every one of you that helped propel this project along towards completion. To you, for being my rock, even when I unfairly expected it of you. I know you would try to give me the moon if I asked for it. To my spiritual teacher, the other me, who waits patiently back home, thank you. For all my brilliant editors – thank you. To Shirley, for reading those first few drafts and always sending love. To Nicky, who always believed, thank you for the messages, especially the ones that were difficult to receive. And my Anna, whose gentle nudges helped me unfold the pages until the perfect ending was found. To Doug, for climbing inside of my head and somehow taking those images and turning them into a breathtaking cover. To Mandy, for the package that saved me. To Michelle, for all the Friday nights spent in tears on your couch. To Vanessa, for all your gentle encouragement and honesty, thank you. To my beautiful daughter Keonna, who joined me early on in my journey, before I had done a lot of healing. Hopefully when you read this you will forgive me for not being a better mother. To my twin girls, who inspire me every single day. To my son, who gives me hope for the next generation of men, telling me at age four "Mommy, I am a protector." To my old friends, thank you for all the times you carried me. To my old friends who are no longer in my life, thank you for playing your part so beautifully. To my new friends, I am so excited to have you on this journey with me, thank you. To everyone who is reading this, thank you. I wrote a section of this book when I was barely 16 and never quite imagined it would actually make it out of my journal and into your hands. Although, I do believe that whoever needs to read this will definitely find a copy, somehow. And finally, to my younger self, for actually living this story and not just writing it. Thank you for never giving up. I have so much compassion and love for you. So much gratitude! I love you all.

About the Author

Shawnda Chambers is a writer and Holistic Nutritionist who runs workshops out of her home in Mono, Ontario.

She can be contacted by email at:
shawndachambers@gmail.com

Made in the USA
Middletown, DE
27 June 2021

42868874R10109